To Cheryl
on Mother's day
1999

from Ron, Faun

Mothers'
Miracles

Other books by
Jamie C. Miller, Laura Lewis, and Jennifer Basye Sander

Christmas Miracles

The Magic of Christmas Miracles

Mothers' Miracles

Magical True Stories of Maternal Love and Courage

Jamie C. Miller, Laura Lewis, and
Jennifer Basye Sander

WILLIAM MORROW AND COMPANY, INC.

NEW YORK

A Big City Books Idea

Grateful acknowledgment is made to reprint the following:

"Crisis at Cape Cod" by Joan LeSueur Woods, copyright © 1995 The Church of
Jesus Christ of Latter-day Saints. First published in *The Ensign*.
Used by permission.

"The Victory," originally published as "Still Enough to Listen"
copyright © 1998 by Intellectual Reserve, Inc. Used by permission.

It is the policy of William Morrow and Company, Inc., and its imprints and affiliates,
recognizing the importance of preserving what has been written, to print the books
we publish on acid-free paper, and we exert our best efforts to that end.

Library of Congress Cataloging-in-Publication Data
Mothers' miracles : magical true stories of maternal love and courage
/ [edited by] Jamie C. Miller, Laura Lewis, and Jennifer Basye Sander. — 1st ed.
p.   cm.
ISBN 0-688-16622-9 (alk. paper)
1. Mothers—Religious life. 2. Miracles. I. Miller, Jamie C.
II. Lewis, Laura, 1963– . III. Sander, Jennifer Basye, 1958– .
BL625.68.M68   1999
306.874'3—dc21   98-43268 CIP

Printed in the United States of America

First Edition

1 2 3 4 5 6 7 8 9 10

BOOK DESIGN BY JO ANNE METSCH

www.williammorrow.com

To mothers everywhere—may your lives be filled with miracles, great and small.

CONTENTS

CONTENTS

CONTENTS

CONTENTS

Where there is great love there are always miracles.
—WILLA CATHER

Mothers'
Miracles

INTRODUCTION

miracle n. 1. *An event that seems impossible to explain by natural laws and so is regarded as supernatural in origin or as an act of God.* 2. *One that excites admiration or awe.*
— WEBSTER'S II RIVERSIDE DICTIONARY

HIS COLLECTION OF true stories is a gift of love, a gift from mothers around the world whose lives have touched and been touched by their children in remarkable ways. These are stories of miracles, large and small, that have grown out of the extraordinary bond between mother and child—bonds so enduring they have sometimes outlasted life itself.

Why a book about mothers and miracles? Because in many ways, the two words are synonymous: every phase of a mother's life is sprinkled with quiet miracles. To begin with, ask any woman who has had difficulty conceiving, and you will appreciate the absolute miracle in that singular event. To be a part of the creation process is, indeed, a most holy calling. And then there is the experience of pregnancy itself, the body's miraculous preparation for a new life. Not only is it a glorious transformation, but the months of carrying a little life wrapped up under your heart is perhaps also the coziest time in a mother's existence.

And who can deny the miracle of birth itself? Having a tiny newborn child placed in your arms is like receiving a personal message from God that the world should go on. Sometimes the infant isn't completely perfect—often not beautiful, occasionally having problems, illness, even deformities . . . but none of that matters. There is simply nothing more breathtaking than that bald, toothless, wrinkled little bundle nestled under your chin. Looking at his radiant face as he sleeps, you are certain that he is not only the most beautiful baby ever born, but is also a miraculous gift. Your life will never be the same again—this little child will reinvent your entire world.

Then you watch in awe as your child grows into maturity. As you fill your days with teaching, nurturing, and kissing away tears, you see the miraculous evolution from baby to child, child to adult. You have the privilege of helping unwrap this precious gift, of enabling your child to see the riches he possesses.

But then there are times when you witness other kinds of miracles along the way—miracles that are not so easily explained away as part of the natural course of life. There is the miracle of a mother who instinctively knows that her son, thousands of miles away, is in danger and prays that his life be spared. There is the miracle of a mother who saves her drowning child during an eerie calm in the ocean's waves. And for the mother unable to conceive and bear her own children, there is the miracle of adoption, as the priceless gift is lovingly passed from one woman's arms to another.

And there are quieter miracles, too: a mother who is able to ease a child's fear, to whisper a word of hope; the miracle of seeing your baby take her first step and later, ride her bike without training wheels; the miracle of hearing your child read his first story out of a book; the miracle of a teenager who returns strong and triumphant from one of life's challenges.

As the cycle of life continues, another miracle occurs: through the daily demands and trials of motherhood, you are humbled. You learn that there is someone else on earth more important than yourself, for whom you would sacrifice almost anything. At first, even *you* are a bit surprised by your unhesitating response that, if needed, you would gladly lay down your life for this little person.

IN OUR HOLIDAY miracle books—*Christmas Miracles* and *The Magic of Christmas Miracles*—we hoped to infuse readers with the sense that, at Christmastime, anything is possible. And what truly matters during that season is not gift giving, but love giving. In this, our third collection of miracle stories, we have collected mothers' accounts of love giving that range from the seemingly ordinary to the otherworldly.

When we began speaking to mother after mother in an effort to gather inspiring stories for *Mothers' Miracles*, we became aware of another theme unfolding—that the love, strength, and courage of mothers can overcome almost any obstacle placed in the path between a mother and her child; once again, the sense that in this realm, anything is possible. The power of motherhood, it seems, is often greater than the laws of nature.

Surely the driving force behind these miracles of mother-hood is love. A mother loves her children fiercely, irra-tionally at times, even when others think they don't deserve to be loved. She is convinced her children are brighter, pret-tier, and more talented than perhaps they really are. Against all the awkward knocks of an awkward world around them, her love is a shield, a guide, a gift. She will be there for them when no one else will.

To a child, every mother's smile is a small prayer, a silent blessing she bestows upon her little ones. Every mother's kiss contains a sprinkling of angel dust that showers a protective circle around them. Mothers are truly earth angels, here to watch over and defend their offspring. And sometimes moth-ers can return later as angels, still guiding their children to peace and safety, even though they themselves cannot be here on earth to insure it.

While researching this book we learned of an incredible tale, just one example of the miracles between mothers and their children. It is the story of Esther Raab, still living today. A young Jewish woman in Europe during World War II, Esther was imprisoned in a concentration camp. Along with the other inmates, Esther planned to participate in a large-scale escape from the camp, Sobibor. The night before the escape, as Esther lay sleeping, her deceased mother appeared to her in a dream.

"Mother, tomorrow I will try to escape!" Esther told her mother in the dream.

"I know that!" her mother replied. "And I've come to tell you where to hide so you'll be safe. After you escape, return to our village. Hide in the barn at the edge of town, the one that you and your brother used to play in. You will be safe there."

Esther did escape from Sobibor, she did make it back to her village, and she at last found the barn her mother described. But inside the barn, Esther suddenly understood the purpose of her mother's urgent words in the dream. For there, hiding beneath the rafters, she discovered her long-lost brother—cold, hungry, afraid, but alive. And in that barn, thanks to the loving guidance of a mother who watched over her children from a world beyond, Esther and her brother hid safely together until the end of the war.

FROM THE MOMENT an infant first clasps his tiny fist around his mother's finger, that mother knows both the unspeakable joy and the heavy burden of her calling. She also knows it is something she'll never regret. With her baby holding tightly on to one of her hands, she reaches up and puts her other hand in the hand of God.

And then she waits for miracles.

—JAMIE, LAURA, AND JENNIFER

Except on Sundays

N MY MEMORIES of my mother, I always seem
to be playing the role of the audience, sitting
in the front-row seats. Every time I think of her now, my
heart sits right down in the very same place, paying the same
sort of attention it always has.

One day when I was a child, my mother sat at her makeup
table wearing my father's plaid bathrobe, her lovely face
copied three times in the triptych mirror. She picked up her
heavy hairbrush as she watched me watch her images. Steam
from the tub was floating toward her out of the bathroom,
carrying the perfume of the bath she had just taken, and I was
sitting on the bed, my legs not yet long enough for my feet to
touch the floor. It's important to the story of my mother to
picture her like this—there, in that funny, dreamy way. It
puts her in context, I think.

"You know, darling," she said, caressing her hair more than

brushing it, "the world of women is divided into two categories."

The steam was coming to her, ghosting right past me through the room.

"Those who believe Rhett came back," she said, passing the brush through her auburn hair, "and those who don't care."

My mother's name was Allene. She is a descendent of the Revolutionary War hero Ethan Allen, and so her parents gave her their own form of the family name. As a child she was a tomboy. In college, she studied journalism. She graduated and became the society editor of the *Long Island Star Journal*, a New York daily newspaper that folded in the 1950s.

She became a wife and mother, a Girl Scout leader, and a visiting nurse volunteer, and after my sister and I were raised, she went back to school and got a master's degree in education and began teaching at a Montessori preschool on the Lower East Side of Manhattan. That puts her in context, too: lovely, but gritty.

Then, sometime in the 1970s, my mother's mind went to battle with something and lost. I used to say that she was losing her mind in handfuls. It was the best description I could think of for what was happening.

She became forgetful, angry, hostile, and incompetent. What began as a daily search for her keys soon became a daily rage in which she would dump the contents of her purse in the middle of the living room floor and shriek that she was losing her mind. She hallucinated wildly. She became violent and had to be sedated. She was fifty-one years old.

When we finally got a diagnosis, the doctor began by saying, "Your mother is not going to die." I thought the words were being offered as comfort and reassurance. Instead, they were preparing us for a diagnosis of long-term care. It was Alzheimer's disease, and it would change all of our lives forever.

By the time she was fifty-six years old, Allene had to be placed in a nursing home. We had run out of options. My father was dead, and my sister and I were in our twenties, working full-time and supporting Allene's twenty-four-hour-a-day, seven-day-a-week home care.

At that point there was very little that seemed to interest her, very little that made her respond. She could no longer speak. She didn't recognize me or my sister. And while we still did things together, she seemed uninterested in anything but watching television and smoking.

Except on Sundays, when we went to church. I have to say right here that we did not go to church out of faith. I had very little faith in anything at that point. We were six years into her illness and what faith I had retained had been mangled by the relentlessness of her disease. We went to church because it was the only place where, for one precious hour each week, she was calm. I seem to recall thinking about converting to Catholicism because I'd heard that the masses were longer.

The church we attended was the Community Church of Douglaston, the church where my mother had been baptized, and where my sister and I had been baptized. It's one of the first buildings you see when you enter the pretty town in which we were raised. We would sit there each Sunday, and in the quiet I would breathe deeply and rest. People were very nice to us there. It had all the comforts of home.

On the last day before she went into a nursing home, I took my mother to church as usual. She had no idea that the next day she was being moved out of the town she loved. I was bereft, feeling guilty and grief-stricken, angry and exhausted and alone.

I remember leaning my head against the side of the pew and weeping. And then I noticed that my mother was singing all the hymns. Probably she had done this every Sunday, but I had never really noticed. And then she said all the words of the Lord's Prayer. This from a woman who could not speak my name.

Years later, after writing about my mother in a book and in several magazine articles, and working as an advocate for people with Alzheimer's disease, I got involved with The Eddy, now a part of Northeast Health, which is an adult-care facility in Troy, New York. I was called to a meeting to create a plan for senior services in the area. A man who was a minister said, "I have always been interested in pursuing the spiritual life of Alzheimer's patients." The memory of my mother in church—her prayers and her ability to sing hymns—flooded my mind. I started to weep.

I realized that without that one hour each week with my mother, I might have gone mad myself. No one can say what that one hour did for my mother, but I believe it was a real blessing. Now that she was gone, other patients and other caregivers needed that blessing, too.

Without meaning to do so, we deny patients the right to worship at the moment they and their family members need it most. When someone cannot sit still or be quiet or remain continent, we discourage their presence in our houses of worship. We may not mean to, but we do—because we don't want someone disrupting the ceremony and spiritual solitude of worship.

So that autumn in Troy, we planned a service around the time and theme of the harvest. We celebrated with a rabbi, an Episcopal priest, and a Presbyterian minister, and intermingled the themes of Sukkoth from the Jewish tradition with Christianity's harvest hymns and prayers. We invited patients and their caregivers. I wrote a prayer for the caregivers and one for the patients. We convinced a priest to keep his sermon under five minutes, used a lot of music, and encouraged walking around throughout the service.

When it came time for the offertory, we circulated baskets of apples; instead of collecting money, we hoped to give something to the patients and their families. The whole idea of the service was to be thankful for what we had, as opposed to focusing on what we had lost to the illness.

From patient to patient, I carried a huge African basket filled with apples. One very ill woman was furled in a wheelchair, her head slumped on her chest, her hands tightened into the gnarls we associate with the very last days of life. Her caregiver shook her head, indicating that the woman would not be able to hear or understand me, but I wanted the old woman to have an apple. I got down on my knees and tried to make eye contact. It was impossible. I tried to open one of her hands, but it was like a knot.

At that moment the offertory hymn began. The opening bars of "How Great Thou Art" came onto the organ, and my husband, an accomplished baritone, softly began singing the hymn.

The woman uncurled. She straightened up in her wheel-chair. At the top of her lungs, she sang every word, with the same clarity my mother had.

The caregiver gasped. I literally staggered back, then watched as the joy and triumph of the lost self of this woman revealed itself to us. She sang from her heart. As the song ended, she curled back into her chair.

We had reached her.

She had reached us, too, as together we saw for ourselves what we knew to be true: that there, amid what had seemed like darkness, was light we had almost overlooked. The same glimmer I had seen in my mother years before.

Emily Dickinson says, "Hope is the thing with feathers." That being the case—and if Emily says it's so, it is—then faith is a thing that can surely fly.

—Marion Roach Smith
Petersburgh, New York

Another Sleepless Night

I DO NOT FALL asleep easily; I never have. Night after night I lie awake next to my husband, Louis, as he sleeps. Sometimes I review the events of the day in my mind, going over small things that happened at work, or thinking about larger things going on in the world around me. Often I think about my three children. And when I do finally fall asleep, my mind is filled with vivid dreams. One of those dreams woke me up one night, and as it turns out, it was for a very good reason.

Scott was my middle child. He was a delightful child, very independent and capable. Our family spent a great deal of time with one another when the children were young; we liked nothing better than a good long camping trip together at our lake lot or at other neighboring lakes. Scott was a master camper, very sure of himself in the woods, in the water, and with our small boat.

It was clear during his high school years that he would probably not go on to college, and his father and I hoped Scott would find his way toward a trade he could master. When he announced his intention of joining the air force after graduation, we couldn't have been more pleased. Louis had been in the air force, too, and was proud that his son planned to follow in his footsteps. True to Scott's independent nature, he took the bus on his own the 230 miles from our town of Aberdeen to Sioux Falls for his physical. I worried that he was too young to be off on his own, but he had other ideas.

Years later, I worried again when he announced that he planned to live in Alaska. Alaska? So far from home in South Dakota? But Scott was determined and excited about his new life in Alaska, and I gradually put my fears aside. It turns out that Alaska is not really so far from South Dakota—we've visited there four times now, and I understand why my son has such love for that beautiful state. A devoted outdoorsman, Scott carries on the camping traditions our family started in his childhood.

And that was Scott's life in Alaska up until the night I had my dream. As I try to recall the circumstances of that night, I can't remember too many details of the dream. All I know is that I was suddenly awake in the middle of the night with a terrible fear about Scott's safety. Louis slept soundly as I lay there in bed, my heart racing. My child was in danger, I just knew it!

He needed my help. How could I help my son in Alaska from my bedroom in South Dakota? There was only one answer: I could pray.

I climbed quietly out of bed and knelt down next to it. I prayed for God to protect my son Scott, to keep him safe and deliver him from harm. I prayed for just a short while, pleading over and over for Scott's life. At last, emotionally drained, I climbed back into bed.

A day or two afterward, I received a call from Scott's former wife, who was in Alaska. "Donna, I need to tell you about something that's happened to Scott. He is in the hospital recovering from a plane crash that happened out in the wilderness." She assured me that he was stable, that I didn't need to bother to come. But once again, I felt that I should be there.

A few days later, we stood next to my injured son's hospital bed. As he grew stronger he was able to tell me the details of what had happened: while he and his friend Gary were returning from a moose hunting trip in the wilderness, their plane was caught upon takeoff by a wind shear. The plane skidded on its belly to a stop and burst into flames. Although Gary had been able to climb out quickly, Scott's seat belt buckle had jammed. As he frantically tried to free himself, he suddenly felt a powerful hand on his shoulder assisting him. Finally free and able to get a safe distance away from the plane, Scott turned to thank Gary for saving him. "Save you?" Gary replied, "I was thirty feet away, rolling on the ground. I never went near the plane!"

I was amazed and humbled. While my son was trapped in a burning plane I had sent him the only help I could: a mother's prayers. Although it would take many months of painful treatment before Scott's injuries were fully healed, he credits the love and support of his family and friends with helping him through the ordeal. And as for me, when I feel the urge to pray for one of my children, I get right on it!

—DONNA WEBER
Aberdeen, South Dakota

The Day I Was Touched
by Snowflakes

*T*HE MORNING OF December 6 changed my life. We had a ranch in the high desert of Nevada, tucked into the fertile plain of an exquisite granite mountain range. We had lived there for two years, but it was like a foreign land to me from the start. I had lived in suburban California all my life. I thought I was fairly worldly, and as it turned out, that was part of the problem.

First impressions are often accurate, often naive, and mine was a little of both. I will never forget driving into the sparsely inhabited community that first week of September. We passed three bars, one post office, and a diner. When we turned left at Shorty's market to get to our ranch, the sign outside the market caught my eye: BEER—ICE—WORMS.

Now, I have a theory that you can tell much about a place by what its market carries. The beer and ice didn't surprise me, but the worms gave me pause. I thought California cuisine was gutsy, so to speak, but this was going a little too far. Was this their regional fare, like grits and chitlins in the South? How do they cook the worms, I wondered?

But in the spring, when the snow melted and the creek ran full, I realized that everyone fished! The worms were bait. I had spent that winter curiously looking into the faces of my new neighbors and driving slowly by their lighted homes in the dark winter nights, wondering if they were eating fried worms. And in fact, as I later got to know some of my neighbors, I suspected some were frying and eating the little critters after all.

But our family was strange to them, too. We were Californians, after all, which was only one step away from being Commies. Our shoes were weird. On top of that, we were employers, always a suspicious group. So for two years, no one really talked to me or played with my children. We were the outsiders in a beer-drinking, worm-eating, xenophobic flock.

To add to my sense of isolation, my husband worked sixteen-hour days and frequently traveled out of state. Yes, I was definitely a lonely stranger in a very strange land. So far, the only winter amusement for my two little boys, other than my giving birth to daughter Ellie in November, was to drive to town and walk slowly through the hardware store playing with the PVC pipes and fittings, flashlights, and keys. On special days we went to Payless drugs for a bag of potting soil, which I brought home and dumped into the empty bathtub. My boys loved it, trucks, shovels, and all. Thank heavens— it gave me a few minutes to myself. I didn't have the use of a TV to serve as an occasional baby-sitter; despite all the millions of miles of wide open sky, the TV waves always got jangled in the cottonwoods nearby and nothing made it to the screen. Not even *Sesame Street*. Alas, my children and I were our own best friends.

On December 6 we had our first snow. Overnight our modest little ranch house was held hostage by thousands of acres of white snow, and the full impact of our move from the city hit me. My husband had always dreamed of ranching, but what was *I* doing here? I was hours from any type of familiar civilization, much less conversation. I mean, I'm always game for a new adventure, but solitary confinement with three little people who didn't speak English as I knew it made me wonder if I had taken this loyalty thing a bit far.

I stared out my kitchen window. I could see for a hundred miles—solid white. Not a fluff or a ruffle. It was as if someone had erased all known landmarks on a map. My view looked like a giant white page, and written in big frosty script were the words: *You're stuck, sister.*

Here I was, alone with a two-week-old nursing baby and two adorable but demanding boys; my husband was still out of town; the dirt drive was covered in deep snow. I hadn't slept more than two hours at a time for a week. I loved my children from the depths of my soul, but I had limits, and this morning was one of those mornings when my limits were being seriously tested.

My two-year-old, David, had an "accident" while wearing my new fuzzy slippers. Roger, four, was flying off the walls, testing decibel levels. Our dog, Rosie, had dragged a soft cube of butter from the kitchen table through the dining room into the living room. She had one paw on the paper while her tongue chased the slippery fat over the new wool rug.

With my fingers covered in butter, I raced to the kitchen to answer the phone while trying to comfort David's sobbing. Somehow over the racket of the drum Roger pounded, I deciphered the message from my husband, calling from sunny California. He wasn't coming home tonight as promised, and wasn't sure when he could be home.

My eyes glazed over. I went numb. Hysterically numb. I felt my way hand over hand to the back door, grabbed my coat, and escaped into the white silence of my yard. I pulled up my collar against the frosty air and negotiated the icy steps, anxious to be immersed in the void. I marched down the drive; the crunch of the snow beneath my feet was the only sound in the world. Suddenly, becoming very self-conscious of my crazy state amid such silence, I lifted my eyes from the drive and . . . froze in my tracks.

I saw what the Indians call *poconip*. When it is very cold with no clouds and no moisture in the air, the earth itself becomes crystallized. Every speck of moisture on each twig, blade, and wisp becomes a starry ice crystal. The trees, fences, and weeds exploded into fireworks of dazzling diamonds in the sunshine. The earth, covered in its awesome splendor, was so bright and clean and sharp my eyes watered from the brilliance. It was the most glorious sight I had ever seen.

I reached down with my ungloved hand and reverently touched the snow. I brought it close to my eyes: lo and behold, I saw a perfect snowflake the size of a pencil eraser on my fingertip. I spread out the other crystals in my palm, and they, too, were tiny perfect snowflakes, each with a different precise pattern. I lifted my eyes to the mountains in front of me—a zillion crystals had anointed them as well. Awestruck and mesmerized, I turned around and slowly walked into the backyard.

I wondered how many people would notice the exquisite pageantry in their own yards that day. The world was covered with diamonds, and almost no one would even realize it. The splendor of it made me feel grand and meek all at the same time—grand because I recognized the pure order of God's creation, meek because it was too glorious to comprehend. A silent song of beauty embraced me; I was royalty.

Once I felt that sense of importance, my perspective changed and joy calmed my spirit. I walked back into the house thrilled, dumbfounded, but most of all, peaceful. I was ashamed by the triviality of my worries, the shortness of my understanding. I had been transformed: everyone looked different to me and everything took on new meaning. I suddenly adored the freckled cheeks and loving eyes of the faces welcoming me back inside. Surely my jubilant heart could find some patience and good humor on a day filled with snowflakes!

I quietly hugged each child, peeked in on my sleeping baby, gave Rosie a few loving ear scrunches. As I looked into their sweet faces, I felt the contentment of the morning as it should be.

While I never knew many of the people in our town, reverence for my world grew within me after that day and sustained my soul. From the grandeur of the lightning storms and exciting prairie fires at night, to the great blue herons and stately deer feasting on apples before the snows, I never felt alone.

I shared the miracle of creation with my children as we

explored this new, wondrous land during those two years. In time we moved to asphalt and concrete towns, so we turned our vision inward to our own gifts—we looked at our lives with a jeweler's eye in the quest to find joy in beauty. It's a struggle sometimes, but whenever life begins to get me down, I think back with gratitude on that miraculous *poconip* morning—the morning that gave me new vision as a mother and brought me closer to home.

—HILARY HINCKLEY
Sacramento, California

Cori's Beads

 BELIEVE IN MIRACLES, some as subtle as a butterfly kiss, some so bold that the air seems to leave the room. My miracle is my daughter, Cori. Although she is gone, she brought me back to life.

Cori was born July 10, 1975. As I held her in my arms that first time I knew immediately there was something different and special about her. Her handmade birth announcement read: "A miracle, and we thought all babies were alike." I didn't understand the prophecy behind those words until years later.

Cori grew into a beautiful child, adapting well to all the changes in life's rich pageant. But our family had its struggles, and when Cori was six, her father and I divorced. Not long afterward, I fell into a life of addiction. As Cori grew, it broke her heart to see her own mother increasingly drawn into the insidious world of drugs, cons, and welfare. Sickness was all I could offer her at that time, yet she never wavered in her love for me. And through her own strength she rose above the mire of my life and walked her own path. At the age of sixteen, she was amazing—she was a cheerleading instructor, an excellent student, and dreamed of becoming a lawyer. Even in my drug-induced fog, I was fiercely proud of her.

I believe God doesn't take anyone until their life's work is completed. Cori died on her birthday. She was one of eight teenagers who died on a sparkling summer day of horsing around in the sunshine. A head-on collision killed them all on their way back home. The accident was so brutal that I was the only mother who was allowed to see her child one last time, lying there in the coroner's office.

A frostbitten numbness descended on me and followed me throughout her funeral. I sat alone with her coffin, and my tears seemed to fall through eternity. Lost in pain, I wanted desperately to pray. But after years of hard living, I had forgotten how.

It would be a neat and tidy story to say that Cori's death sobered me up. But that is not what happened. When the numbness of shock started to wear off I redoubled my drug taking, seeking to deaden my feelings the best way I knew how. My life continued in a downward spiral. There were several more years of addiction before I finally sought treatment.

But seek treatment I did, and with each day away from drugs my head cleared and I walked a little closer to both reality and spirituality. And in this healing environment "things" started to happen for me, little miracles that orbited around my daughter, Cori.

After graduating from Crutchers Serenity House, I stayed

on to work with other addicts. I was terrified of this new role, but I had begun to turn to God for direction. The more my spirituality grew, the more I evolved. I had begun my journey.

One of the stops on my journey was the very coroner's office in which I'd last seen Cori. As I worked to undo the damage I'd left in the wake of my addiction, I sought to give back in some small way through community service. The coroner's office was the last place Cori had been, and I was both sickened and compelled by the place. But God had sent me here so that I might be better prepared to counsel others in the same position I had been in many years before—a distraught parent facing the ultimate loss.

When the coroner gently explained that he had been there when they brought Cori in, I knew why I was there. I learned everything about how she died. That she died quickly was important for me to know. That she had not been drinking meant a great deal to me. It bolstered my deep desire to have her be proud of me, too. I prayed that, wherever she was, she could see me.

Wanting so much to feel her presence again, I went to visit the accident site. The spot on the road had been marked with eight crosses, each one dedicated to the special life that was now gone. I stood frozen at the sight that greeted me—after all these years, Cori's cross was the only one still standing. The vision of this struck me deeply, and I started to pray. I prayed for some kind of connection, any kind of connection, with my lost daughter. My heart ached as I prayed, reliving those last moments in the coroner's office with her lifeless body. Surely her soul had soared free at this very place as her body had died. Where was that soul now?

As I stood quietly praying, my body swayed slightly. I spread my feet quickly to regain my balance, and I heard a faint crunch from under one foot. I looked down at the ground. There was something sticking out of the dirt. I bent down for a closer look and brushed away the dirt to reveal a faded string of rosary beads. Cori's rosary beads.

Filled with awe and gratitude at God's compassionate sign, I began to cry. Cori was with me. She was watching over me then, and she continues to show herself to me now. Cori appears in the faces of the troubled young women I counsel, in that moment when I see their eyes light up with hope and promise. She comes to me when my spirit is low and breathes a warm glow into my heart. She brings me the people who were a part of her life—friends in trouble who mercifully cross my path. She is all around me, and the most important miracle is that, today, I finally know that.

— CHRIS LLOYD
Deer Park, California

Crisis at Cape Cod

I T WAS A sweltering July afternoon on the Cape Cod beach at Woods Hole, Massachusetts. On the horizon a couple of thunderheads rumbled, but the rushing of the waves and the music of the children's voices orchestrated a feeling of peace. I watched my two children, three-year-old Vickie and four-year-old Greg, scampering at the water's edge. My friend's son Ralph, a tall, slim nine-year-old, was digging for sand crabs.

"What time is it?" my friend Mary Allen asked.

"It's two-thirty." I watched as Greg plopped down onto a red plastic raft. My gaze followed his short legs as he paddled in the shallow water.

I turned to Mary Allen for a second as she began to speak: "I'm going to the house . . ." I lost the rest of her sentence as a sudden premonition chilled me. Instantly, I was alert. Where was the raft?

I ran toward Ralph. "Where's Greg?" I asked.

"He was just on the raft and floated out . . ." Ralph squirmed as he floundered for words.

Greg's life jacket lay on the sand, discarded where I had last seen him playing. Frightened, Vickie started to cry. "Didn't see him take it off," she began.

Then I spotted the raft—fifteen feet offshore, rocking back and forth like an empty cradle. "Greg!" I shouted against the wind, panic in my voice. Quickly I scanned the beach—no sign of his curly blond hair. Again and again I called out, nearly paralyzed by fear. No reply.

For the third time in less than two minutes, Ralph and I combed the entire cove. Greg had vanished.

Sprinting up to me, Ralph said quietly, "Police?"

"It's hopeless," I replied, trying to stay calm. "They'd never make it in time."

Vickie screamed, "Greg's drowning!"

Shaking, I felt my teeth chatter as my pulse pounded in my ears. I tried to reassure them. "We'll find him," I said. Yet as I spoke, my voice sounded hollow. Greg had had a few swimming lessons, but not enough to be proficient.

Mentally I counted the minutes. It was now two thirty-five. A friend's son had drowned recently; I knew that the brain could survive only four to six minutes without oxygen. I pictured him floating lifeless on the water. Instinctively, I drew a deep, jagged breath for Greg. I couldn't give up! Yet the more I looked, the more discouraged I felt. How could he disappear in seconds?

Terror shot through me. If I don't find Greg immediately, he'll be gone in thirty seconds, I thought. Despair threw me into a depth lower than I thought possible. But I pushed the negative images away and prayed as I ran: "Heavenly Father, help me find him—please."

An eerie tingling surged up my spine as the water seemed suddenly to go still, motionless like smooth, cold glass. There was silence, and the atmosphere was charged with electricity and white light—it seemed like the aura in a bolt of lightning. I held my breath.

At that moment, I saw tiny fingertips sticking out of the surface of the water, fifteen feet from the shore. Gasping at the icy water, I plunged into the sea with my eyes wide open—afraid that I might lose sight of my son's fingers. Without warning, I was slammed back by a wall of frigid water that locked me in its hammering, suffocating grip. Thinking of the horrible death that awaited Greg if I failed, I continued to pray: "Don't let him die!" I blinked. Greg's fingers were still there. I swam with long strokes.

At last I reached him. Although his limp body was turning blue, he was on his toes, struggling to get to the crest of the waves, fighting for life while the undercurrent pulled him down. I towed him back to shore. His eyelashes fluttered; he opened his eyes, coughed, and then breathed.

"Mamaaa," he finally cried. His breath came in shudders. I felt the Spirit's presence as I hugged my son with relief.

More than ten minutes had elapsed between the time I discovered him missing and the moment I lifted him out of the sea. I was told later that if the water had been above seventy degrees Fahrenheit, he would have suffered brain damage; but because the water had been so cold, he had survived without any injury.

I know the Lord continues to perform miracles, and just as He calmed the Sea of Galilee two thousand years ago, He calmed the ocean during my crisis at Cape Cod.

—DR. JOAN LeSUEUR WOODS
Mesa, Arizona

No Greater Love

A CRY IN THE night from my two-year-old daughter jolted me awake for the third night in a row. As I entered her room, Marissa was sitting on her bed, holding her head and crying. Between sobs she repeatedly told me that her head was "ouchie."

I was beginning to doubt the assumption I had made several days earlier. Life in our house had been hectic. I had recently opened my own business and was busy preparing for a new baby to arrive in six weeks. Our two girls were also adapting to having a sitter all day while Mommy was working. It was enough to make a thirty-year-old feel like crying and holding her head, too. I had naturally assumed that Marissa was just craving a little extra attention. Now, however, I was worried.

The next morning and throughout the day, Marissa continued to complain about her head. Her medical checkup was only a few days away, but I decided that I would call the doctor to discuss my concern. The nurse suggested that if the headaches continued, I should mention them to the doctor during Marissa's checkup.

On February 6, 1997, I explained the situation to the doctor. As I watched him proceed with his examination, I became concerned as he performed simple reflex tests on Marissa's toes not once or twice but several times. He also seemed to spend a great deal of time shining a light in her eyes. A few minutes later, I sat and listened. The doctor explained that headaches in two-year-olds were not very common. Given this fact, coupled with some poor reflex response during Marissa's exam, he wanted to do some tests to rule out anything more serious—including a brain tumor. Just being cautious, he assured me. The MRI procedure that he was requesting would essentially allow the doctors a peek inside her brain. "Brain tumors in children are very rare," he repeated.

After arriving home and calling my husband, David, I immediately called Marissa's grandma, Barb. "Stepmother" never seemed to convey the warmth of the special relationship that Barb and I shared. I was only fourteen when my mother passed away. Looking back, I am impressed at how my father raised three teenage girls alone through the next six years. Although I still longed for my mother, I was a little unsure when my dad remarried in 1987. We'd have to share him with Barb and her two children.

But over the years I discovered a special kind of relationship with Barb. I now had a special mom to do things with, to help plan my wedding, to rush to the hospital when I gave birth, and to love my children as her own grandchildren. I had someone I could talk to about my own mother, someone to share special occasions, and someone to watch over my father. During this difficult time with Marissa, Barb did much to encourage and support me, even though she was dealing with her own bad headache from a sinus infection.

The next week, the strain of waiting for the MRI appointment, fear of the unknown, the daily stress of caring for two little ones, coupled with the raging hormones of pregnancy caused me to crumble one afternoon. I found myself sobbing on the phone to Barb. She, of course, rushed to my house and sat with me and helped to pass the time. She spent time rocking Marissa and reading to both girls. As the girls napped, Barb told me how hard she had been praying that everything would be fine. The possibility of a brain tumor was unthinkable to her. Marissa had not yet lived, Barb said. Then Barb told me she had prayed that if someone should have a brain tumor, it should be her, not Marissa. She had lived a life full of love, marriage, children, and grandchildren.

On January 20, my father and Barb sat together in the waiting room at Children's Hospital as the staff began to prepare Marissa for her MRI. She was difficult to put to sleep, but finally, with an IV, she was asleep, and the procedure began. David stayed in the room with her, but because of my pregnancy, I stayed in the waiting room, where Dad and Barb continued to assure me that things would be fine.

The next morning our doctor telephoned with the results.

I could hear his relief when he told me that the MRI did not show a brain tumor or anything else serious. The MRI did, however, show that Marissa had a severe sinus infection. At her age that would account for the headaches and perhaps for the coordination problems. The good news was that with three weeks of dosing with antibiotic "pink stuff," the headaches would disappear.

Life in our home seemed to return to normal as we prepared for the arrival of our third child in March. As usual, Dad and Barb met us at the hospital for the birth of our son, Thomas. After that, I thought things would finally settle down.

Our annual Easter gathering and Easter egg hunt was held at Dad and Barb's house. Barb was very carefree, but Dad seemed very tense. Something just did not seem right. The whole atmosphere that day was very stressful. Almost immediately after my sisters and I returned to our own homes, we phoned one another to try to figure out what was so terribly wrong. We all agreed that Barb and Dad were both acting strange. The following Monday, Dad asked if we had noticed anything different about Barb. She was not acting normal. It started with little things, like randomly changing the channel on the television, but included more serious incidents like shopping excessively. She was also complaining of a constant throbbing sinus headache.

Their family physician dismissed it all as some sort of depression and prescribed an antidepressant, but the next week things escalated. The odd little behaviors became more bizarre. Dad took her to the doctor who treated her diabetes rather than returning to the family physician. The doctor sent her immediately to the hospital for further testing.

I remember sitting with Barb at the hospital as the neurologist gave her a short simple test. What day was it? What hospital was she in? What floor was she on? Why was she here? Could she remember the following items: cat, book, chair? Somehow I found the strength not to cry in front of Barb when I saw that she couldn't pass the test. I knew in my heart that something was terribly wrong. Like a child, I suddenly wanted to run away to the playground for a place to hide and cry, as I had done almost sixteen years earlier when my mother had died.

The next day, after an MRI, the doctors made the diagnosis: Barb had a massive brain tumor. The doctors figured that it may have started growing sometime in January when her "sinus headaches" began. By now it was very large and would require surgery at the minimum. But Barb did not make it to surgery because the tumor hemorrhaged. My special mom, Barbara Vork Barth, died on April 12, 1997, less than one week after being diagnosed with a brain tumor.

Were the similarities in condition and timing between Barb and Marissa a mere coincidence? Or are there a handful of souls on earth so angelic that they would literally give up their life for someone they loved? I believe my heart knows the miracle in our story, but in either case I am grateful for the rare opportunity to have been loved so deeply by two mothers and to have witnessed their courage and commitment to their families.

Although our girls were only four and two when their grandma died, their love for her was strong. The headaches in the night no longer wake Marissa and no longer frighten me. My new challenge is to remember the example of strength and love as I wipe away my daughters' tears and comfort them as they cry for their grandma.

—JILL E. REED
Columbus, Ohio

Rings on the Water

ASSE, MY SON, has always loved horses. One day he suddenly said with a world of longing in his voice: "I want so much to have a friend in the Wild West of America. I want to see a photo of him sitting on his horse . . ." In Sweden, where we live, you don't see such things.

My husband, Olle, and I looked at each other, our hearts heavy. Only five years old, Lasse had a tumor in his optical nerves and was going blind quickly—in fact, his doctors had warned us there would not be many months before his sight would be gone altogether. Olle and I wanted him to have lots and lots of sights and pictures to remember during the rest of his life: a lifetime of visual pleasures crammed into a few months before total blindness set in.

But an American pen pal with a horse of his own? We had no connection with the Wild West. Where and how could we find Lasse a friend? Even if we could find him a pen pal, how could we make it happen before he lost his sight completely?

Out of nowhere, an idea came to me. I remembered the copy of *Ladies' Home Journal* that I'd bought in the train station a few weeks earlier. Maybe if I wrote a letter to them, perhaps a member of the staff would know someone who might know someone. . . . It was worth a try.

I immediately found some paper and sat down at the kitchen table, Lasse by my side. On a sheet of paper he began to draw a picture for his new pen pal. On another one I wrote a letter to the editor of *Ladies' Home Journal* and explained the situation. Could she help us, please?

We put our two pieces of paper in an airmail envelope, and I dropped it into the mailbox with a silent prayer.

The weeks slipped by. After a while Lasse stopped asking whether any letters had arrived for him. His sight was quickly deteriorating, and I had given up all hope of a pen pal for him when one day the postman dropped four letters into our mailbox. Four letters from America with Lasse's name on them!

We sat down at the kitchen table and opened the letters. Lasse's eyes shone like stars when a photo dropped out of the envelope.

"There it is!" he cried. "There it is! It is a horse! And that is him, my friend—look, he is sitting on his horse!"

Lasse picked up another photo. He looked puzzled, turning it this way and that, trying to decide what he was looking at. He gave the photo to me, but I wasn't sure what it was, either. So I read the accompanying letter: "Dear Lasse," it said, "this is the ear of my hoss, it is a bitt blurd, I toke the pitcher myself. . . ."

Lasse stared at the blurred horse's ear with admiration. "A real ear of a real Wild West horse!" he said, beaming.

A load had fallen from my shoulders with the arrival of these letters. Lasse had had his wish fulfilled—it was a gift from heaven.

But it was only the beginning. The next day twelve letters came. Two days later, another thirty arrived. Lasse was excited. He studied every new photo with great concentration and eagerness, holding them very close to his eyes, using what sight he had left to capture every detail and store them in his memory.

Weeks and months passed and more letters kept coming—touching letters, funny letters, even gifts. Little children sent well-worn toys. Lasse's own favorite toy was a hairless and mended teddy bear, so he knew that these were beloved toys, not rejected ones.

Then the day came when Lasse's sight was gone altogether. Letters continued to arrive, and at first we did not know what to do with them. Would Lasse be depressed because he couldn't see them? I took a chance—I told him that more letters had arrived, and his face lit up. Without hesitation he asked Olle and me to read them aloud and to describe the photos. We soon found that he created new pictures, using details he remembered from all the photos he had seen in the weeks before he went blind, details he wouldn't have known without all of those carefully stored and cherished images.

Even easier to "see" were the gifts that friendly and imaginative people sent to him, things he could feel and touch. In one envelope we found a soft, faded neckerchief, thin with wear. The sender was an elderly lady who told us that she had saved it for over sixty years. She'd been given it as a young girl by a rodeo rider whom she loved very much. She'd kept it all these years, and now she felt it was time to give it away. "I must have kept it for Lasse," she wrote to me, "although I didn't know it until I read about him in the magazine."

Deeply touched by her words, we watched as Lasse unfolded the kerchief very gently, with fingers that touched the thin cloth as lightly as butterfly wings. He put it around his neck, touching it every now and then with a little smile, maybe trying to imagine what the young rodeo rider was like who had worn it sixty years before.

In one package we found a child-size cowboy outfit. The woman who sent it explained that her father had been a child movie star in the beginning of the century and had worn this outfit in many of his films. What generosity—she had given Lasse a memory from her own treasured family history.

In some letters there were flint arrowheads, rattles from rattlesnakes—treasures to touch and feel from a real world thousands and thousands of miles from Lasse's own newly dark world. One day we received a letter from a Native American named Glade Beaver. He sent a picture of his younger brother, sitting on a pinto horse, long black braids hanging over his shoulders. My son's face lit up. How much more western could life be for a small Swedish boy?

It was like rings in the water. With each letter, each item to touch, Lasse's world grew, he found new questions to ask about things that turned his mind to other people, other situations, other parts of the world.

The letters from America continued to arrive for over a year. During the next two years Lasse had brain surgery twice. Each time we moved to be near him in the hospital, and with every move we dragged along the huge trunk where we kept his treasured letters and photos. Whenever he felt low I would take out a few of the letters and read them aloud to him in his hospital room.

And after several years, life finally settled into a fairly normal routine. Lasse was able to attend the regular school near our house instead of a boarding school for blind children. And the boy who loved horses did finally get one of his own. Lasse and his little sister groomed and cared for their horses and rode them every day.

On cold winter evenings, when our world was padded with snow and the days were far too short, our little family would sit together and read from a thick stack of magazines—*The Western Horseman*. An anonymous (but generous) soul had given Lasse a five-year gift subscription!

I have described here just a few of the letters and gifts that our son received in answer to my prayer. There are hundreds of letters in that old trunk—I have it still. Each of the letters was precious, each one gave Lasse joy, comfort, and an exciting feeling of adventure at a time in his life when he needed it badly.

One day over thirty years ago I crossed my fingers and

dropped my son's wish into the mail. A kind editor decided to help an unknown little boy, and what she did worked like a stone dropped into water, spreading rings that grew wider and wider. It was a miracle to us. It still is.

—KERSTIN BACKMAN
Grängesberg, Sweden

The Decision

NOT ALL MOTHERS are blissfully happy when their first child is born. For some, the circumstances are difficult and confusing. That was the case the night my girlfriend dropped me off at St. Anthony's Hospital. Alone and afraid, I was taken to a small room and told to put on a gown and lie on the bed. The nurses didn't speak much to me—I was unmarried, young, alone, and pregnant, and such a thing was frowned upon, especially in the South in the early 1970s. Alone I bore the heaviness of the labor of childbirth in a darkened labor room, only occasionally checked by nurses who didn't show much compassion.

Little did I know of the workings of such a place—of what had already been planned for me. The hospital had a social service director, and when an unmarried, teenage girl came in to give birth, they had a deserving family already in mind for the new child. They would help me see how inadequate and unprepared I was for childbirth, much less for parenthood. And of course they were right.

After my delivery, I woke from a deep sleep. In the dark hours before dawn, I looked around the room: old linoleum yellowed on the floor beneath my railed bed; one small light on the wall behind me; a metal chair against the wall. Where was my baby? Was it a girl, a boy? I cried out, and in my drug-induced state, I vaguely remembered my mother bending over me. "It's a girl," she whispered. "She is healthy and beautiful."

When I awoke some hours later I rang for the nurse and asked for my baby. She seemed puzzled, but after much persistence on my part, she brought in a small bundle and laid her in my arms. The baby was so beautiful, so small, so perfect. Thick, dark curly hair topped her round pink face. Her eyes were as dark as raisins, and her skin was as smooth as the finest silk. A baby! A little person! My mind was swirling with thoughts and my heart overflowing with emotions. I had no idea what I was doing, but this I did know: my life would never be the same.

Soon after, a social worker came to visit me. She explained that they had a family, a special and loving family who had been waiting for so long for a child they could love and care for. She talked to me about responsibility, my future, and the opportunities I would lose trying to raise a baby alone. Much of what she said was true. I was so young—only sixteen years old—but I felt deep in my soul that this was the most important decision I would perhaps ever make.

I told her I would pray. I didn't know much about prayer—I had been to church as a young girl with my grandmother and my mother, but I had no deep religious feelings of my own. There had certainly been times when I had prayed in the past, "Please get me out of this mess!" but I knew this was a different kind of prayer. I needed an answer. I waited for it. I listened. Day after day I listened, with the social worker encouraging me to do the responsible thing for this little girl. Each afternoon, friends visited me, quiet about their opinions. Each evening my mother and grandmother visited, also quiet. Everyone was waiting for me. I was waiting for God.

After nine days the pressure was mounting. The hospital wanted my bed. The social services wanted my baby. I wanted my answer. One afternoon my girlfriend tiptoed into my room. She sat on the side of my bed and took my hand in hers. Eyes brimming with tears, she shared her hidden secret with me. She too had been an unwed, teenage mother. She too had faced this decision. She too had been afraid. In heartbreaking detail she described her feelings and concerns at the time. She knew exactly how I was feeling! She told me that now, at age twenty-one, she knew in her heart that letting go of her baby to a loving and wonderful family had been the right thing to do, and she encouraged me to do the same. She left, and I was alone with my thoughts. I had prayed for God to give me an answer. Was this it? Logically it made sense. It must be right, but what was wrong with my heart? It felt like it was breaking.

That night my mother came again to see me. She had kept her opinions to herself as I had struggled over the past few days, waiting for an answer to my prayers. She knew more, saw more, felt more than she shared with me. It would be many years later when she would confirm the events of that night with me.

The Decision

I had been waiting for her to come. All afternoon I'd cried. I told my mother of the visit with my friend, of the story she had shared. I told her that after talking to my friend I had decided to let my baby go home with the family that waited for her. I had decided in my mind, but what was I going to do about my heart? The feelings there were quite different. I felt as if I was grieving. I felt something had died inside of me.

At last, my mother began to share her feelings with me. She did not agree with my girlfriend and told me of her own impressions over the past several days. I don't remember much of what she said, for I was listening—listening to the sound of my baby crying in the nursery. I got up and walked down the corridor to the baby nursery at the end of a long hall. It didn't occur to me that it would have been impossible for me to hear a baby crying so far away and in an enclosed room, much less to distinguish the sound of my own crying child. But somehow I just knew she was crying and that I needed to go to her.

I was not aware of my mother following me down the hall to the nursery—I was conscious only of the sound of my daughter's cry. Then something happened that even now is almost too miraculous to describe.

As I peered through the glass wall that separated me from my crying child, a bright, white light seemed to descend from the ceiling above her and encompassed the crib in which she lay. It was luminous and shone directly on her little body. Then I heard these words, as clearly as if someone were speaking in my ear. "This is your child. She was sent here to you. No one will ever be able to love her as you will." Suddenly, joy swelled within my heart and peace filled my aching soul, and I knew God had truly heard and answered my prayers. The next morning, a long ten days after her birth, I took my precious daughter home with me.

The years that followed were certainly not easy. I worked as a waitress, spent two years in college, and made many mistakes along the way. I know the decision to keep the baby would not be right for many young women; giving up a baby for adoption is a noble act of love. And yet time after time, the voice I heard and the light I saw that night gave me the courage to know I had done the right thing for this particular baby.

I had been given a clear understanding that this child would need *my* love and devotion in her life. But what soon become even more evident was that I would need *her* love and support to carry me through some difficult years. That daughter has now graduated from college and is making a wonderful life on her own. I cannot imagine what my life would have been without her.

—CINDY BARKSDALE
Amarillo, Texas

Her Only Secret

M Y MOTHER'S PARENTS brought her across the ocean from Italy to America in 1913 when she was only two years old. As the oldest daughter of a large family living in New York City, growing up in hard times, she bore much of the responsibility of caring for her brothers and sisters. As her mother got older, she also took care of her. She loved her mother with a passion that shone through every time she told us stories and showed us pictures of her. I never knew my grandmother, but I felt a strong connection to her through my mother's obvious devotion.

After eleven years of marriage and many miscarriages, my mother finally gave birth to me when she was thirty-eight years old. She always said I was a special gift and miracle from God, and she named me Angela after my grandmother. My mother was a stunning woman with beautiful olive skin and long dark curly hair. Her beauty alone could've brought many opportunities in life, but she was fiercely dedicated to being a wife and mother.

She had some health problems that started in her forties. Poor circulation in her legs made walking difficult for her, but when I began school, she would walk the five blocks to school with me in the morning, return at lunchtime, and then be back to walk me home after school. Thirty blocks a day, in all kinds of weather, by a woman for whom walking was very painful. And she never complained about her life, she only seemed grateful for it.

But the thing that was most important to my mother was education, and she made sure it was to me, also. When she was growing up, education was a luxury that many couldn't afford. Dad's father died when he was young, so he had to quit school after the second grade and work to help his family survive. Mom went to school up to the sixth grade, when she, too, was required to help her family. That's how things were in the 1920s.

From the time I started grammar school, all the way through high school, my mother helped me with my homework. I was a bright, challenging child, and I know I tested her patience often. When I was very young, it never occurred to me how exceptionally smart she was for the amount of education she had received. She seemed to know everything about every subject and could answer any question I had. It didn't matter whether I was studying the Civil War, decimals and fractions, or Mark Twain, she understood whatever I was learning—often better than I did. In our three-room walk-up apartment in the Bronx, I would sit at the kitchen table for hours doing my homework. She would work around the kitchen the whole time, always available to answer any question or help with any project. I just assumed that all mothers were like this, smart and helpful. But as I got a little older, I began to realize how really intelligent she was, and I often wondered where she got all her knowledge.

When I was finishing high school in the 1960s, the rest of the family maintained that it was "a waste for a girl to go to college," my mother stood firm against them. In many ways, she was liberated before her time; she knew that the real opportunities in life would be saved for those with a higher level of education than her own.

As I tried to decide whether or not to attend college, my mother revealed the secret behind her wisdom. And when she told me, in an effort to impress on me the importance of continuing my education, I was touched and very proud.

Every night of my life after I went to bed, my mother would wait until she knew I was asleep and then would quietly come into my room to get my schoolbooks. She would sit at the kitchen table late into the night, reading the next chapter in each of my textbooks so that she could stay just a little ahead of me. As I slept, she secretly taught herself American history, algebra, science, literature—subjects she was learning for the first time in her life—just a night or two before she would confidently discuss them with me.

She tested herself at the end of every chapter to make sure she'd be able to answer all of my questions the next day. She read and reread Shakespeare until she could explain it to me. She developed a love for reading that was contagious and to which I credit any success I've had in life so far. Her example taught me that whatever I didn't know I could always learn from someone else who had written about it in a book.

My mother never used all the knowledge she gained those years as a means for her own employment or for any personal gain. Night after night, she gave up going out, gave up social activities, or working on her own hobbies and interests so that my life would be richer.

Of all the gifts my mother gave me, her tremendous sacrifice of time and energy to make sure her child had a good education is the greatest gift of all. Because of that gift, I have been able to do what I love most in life—to teach and write professionally. Now I am the one who misses her mother, just as my mother missed my grandmother. Now I am the one who tells my daughter stories about the grandmother she never knew, who died just eighteen days before her first birthday.

Pope Paul once said, "Every mother is like Moses. She does not enter the promised land. She prepares a world she will not see." For my mother, and perhaps for most mothers, that preparation was accomplished in the quiet of the night without praise or recognition, but with great sacrifice and love.

— ANGIE MANGINO
Staten Island, New York

Help at Harvest Time

ECAUSE MY FATHER was an alcoholic, my sisters and brother and I clung to our mother while we were growing up. When she was suddenly killed in a car accident at age forty-nine, we were completely unprepared and deeply shaken. My youngest sister, Karen, was only fourteen at the time and was too afraid to go and live with my father, so she came to live with me in Lincoln, Nebraska. For the next eight years, Karen and I shared good times and bad together, always trying to understand why God had taken away our mother—the only stable thing in our lives—when we were so young and so dependent upon her love.

My father died in 1988, and one year later I married a wheat farmer and moved to western Nebraska, about four hundred miles from the home of my childhood. The next few years brought us a wonderful daughter and son, Shannon and Jay. They were a delight to us and did much to fill the emptiness in my heart left by my mother's death. And as the cycle of life naturally unfolds, I would begin to learn things from my children that even my own mother couldn't have taught me.

Farming is a very family-oriented occupation, especially in the month of July, when the wheat is harvested. Since most of the year's income is based on that event, all available members of one's extended family are called upon to help in one way or another during that time. Parents, grandparents, cousins, aunts, and uncles commonly pitch in with cooking, moving vehicles, going for parts during machinery breakdowns, baby-sitting the little ones while wives drive grain carts and trucks, and much more.

For me, harvest time has always been an especially difficult season because I couldn't just pick up the phone and ask "Mom and Dad" to come and help whenever I needed it. Other than my husband's parents, neither of us has any extended family available to assist us during the harvest. As I listened to other farmers talk about their family's involvement, my heart would once again ache for my mother. Sometimes I wondered where she was and what she was doing, and if her heart longed for her children as ours did for her.

One day during this season while my mother-in-law, Barbara, was staying with the children, I went for a walk along the country roads. As I watched the combines and trucks among the wavy golden wheat fields, I wondered if my mother was even aware of my life and the direction it had taken—if she had any idea that I was married, living on a wheat farm, and the mother of two children.

When I walk out in nature, I often like to pray. On this

particular day, I told God that I knew He was busy with so many things in the world, but that if it wasn't too much trouble, could He please send some sort of sign that my mother knew where I was and hadn't forgotten me. I told Him that I knew there were much more important things for Him to think about, but that I would be very grateful for just a little something to let me feel her presence.

A few days later in the evening, I was giving Jay a bottle in the living room when Shannon came in the door. She had just turned three and had been playing in the front yard on her swing set. Shannon is a very normal and active child, but she has never been one to play make-believe much with dolls or toys. When she entered the house, she had an unusually serious look on her face. Very deliberately, she said, "Mommy, your mommy wants to see you."

I said, "What?" Again she said very intently, "Your mommy wants to see you." I was stunned! I looked at her in disbelief as she continued, "Hurry, Mommy, she's waiting!" I got up with Jay in my arms, and as we were going out the door I said, "Where is she?" "She's here!" Shannon replied. "I show you."

We crossed the driveway and went over to the swing set. I said, "Where, sweetie?" She pointed up above the swing set and said, "There, right there!"

I tried to remain calm, but I know my knees were shaking. Shannon very naturally climbed onto her swing while I put Jay in the baby swing and began pushing him. I kept looking around, trying to take in every visible movement, every sound, every brush of wind against my skin. I could hardly breathe.

Trying to act as nonchalant as Shannon, I asked, "Where is she now?" Shannon pointed to the space right beside me and said, "Right there." I was shaken to the core, so stunned I could hardly speak. I wanted so badly to feel her, to talk to her, but in the end all I could utter was a simple "Mom, I love you!"

I suppose that's all that really needed to be said. She was there with me. She knew about my life. She was a friend to my children. She already knew the feelings of my heart. I was sure of it.

This incredible experience lasted about fifteen minutes. Shannon was very calm and unaffected throughout. This was nothing unusual to her. When I finally asked Shannon if my mother was still there she replied, "She's gone now."

Before this event, I had never discussed my mother with Shannon, nor was she even aware that she ought to have another "grandma." Shannon never again brought up what happened that day, but I was completely awed and humbled by this very loving, undeniable answer to a mother's simple prayer. Whenever I think about it, a sense of peace envelops me like a warm blanket. I feel great joy knowing that I have a mother up in heaven who still cares about me, and even more important, that I have a father there, too.

—KRISTIN PETERSON LINTON
Dalton, Nebraska

Mama's Warning

*T*HE GRAND OLD oak tree had stood as a land-
mark at the bustling intersection for more
than five decades. Its spreading branches and huge solid
trunk were a familiar signpost in the local community. And
each day, a parade of children walked past the tree on their
way to St. Mary's Elementary School.

The tree had been there for as far back as I can remember.
It must have been a young tree when the town was settled,
growing tall and strong long before I was born, even long
before my grandparents moved into the neighborhood.

In all those years, the giant oak changed very little. Until
the day when a tragic accident took the life of a young girl
who, like myself, had passed by the tree many times on her
way to school. The accident occurred at the busy intersection
in front of the tree. The girl was struck by a speeding car as
she rushed to school one morning. She was carried by a

passer-by to the shade of the oak tree, where she died of her injuries. Later, someone carved a large cross deep into the bark of the tree to serve as a constant memorial and reminder of that unfortunate day.

Our little community was devastated by the accident. Mama was so unnerved by it that she laid down a new rule: I was not to cross at that busy intersection, nor was I to play near the tree. She took her new rule so seriously that she insisted that I walk the long way around to school to avoid the tree, even though it meant that every morning I had to leave a few minutes earlier for class. When I protested about this inconvenience to my morning routine, she replied, "It is more important to be safe!"

So I obeyed my mother and always took the long route to school. Until the morning when my alarm failed to ring. By the time I awoke I was already five minutes late for final exams. I threw on my clothes, grabbed my books, dashed out the door, and raced toward school. I came to the block where I usually turned to take the long route that Mama insisted upon. *It is more important to be safe!* I stopped my running and stood on the corner for a brief moment, breathing hard and hopping anxiously from one foot to the other while I considered what I was about to do. I made up my mind and raced down the road toward the tree. Despite Mama's warnings, I chose the shortest route. I prayed she would never find out.

Running at top speed, I soon reached the busy intersection. As I stood in front of the tree, impatiently waiting for the traffic to clear, I suddenly heard my mother's voice call out, "Sarah! Sarah! Watch out!" Startled to hear her voice, I spun quickly to look for her behind me and saw a runaway flatbed truck hurtling down the road and headed directly toward me. Without pausing to think, I instinctively jumped behind the big tree for protection. A moment later the flatbed truck crashed head-on into the tree. From my hiding place I could feel the giant tree absorb the blow.

After the crash, trembling, I came out from behind the tree to look for Mama. She must be awfully angry, I thought, to have followed me down the street to scold me for disobeying her . . . Sheepishly I studied all of the faces in the growing crowd, searching for hers. But I could not find her.

Hours later I came home at lunchtime to talk to her. "Where were you this morning?" I asked.

"Right here," she replied. "I've been home all morning."

Whose voice did I hear shout the warning that day, so many years ago? My mother's, of course. For even when their children are far away and out of sight, loving spirits are walking beside us, doing their best to keep us safe and feeling loved. It has been said that God, knowing He couldn't be everywhere, invented mothers. The day I heard Mama's voice, I understood why He had.

— SARAH RIZZOLO CURCI
San Jose, California

Gabby's Touch

DINNERTIME IN A hospital is one of a nurse's busiest hours, but when I got the page from Dr. Clark, I dropped everything. I was pregnant and he was my doctor—I knew it must be important. He told me my alpha-fetoprotein (AFP) level was a little off and that I should have it checked. My mind started racing, going through all the possibilities heralded by abnormal AFP levels: Down's syndrome, spina bifida, twins. And a more serious neural tube defect called anencephaly, the outcome of which, if the baby was carried to term, was death within hours.

When I got home from work, I read about all these conditions in my nursing books, mentally preparing myself for the worst. After hours of poring over the books, I felt I was ready to face whatever the diagnosis might be. If God intended me to have a baby with birth defects, then that's what I would do.

Two days later I was referred to a geneticist, Dr. Hermann.

He started his investigations with an ultrasound. He walked my husband and me through it: "The legs look good—see how they move . . . here's the spinal cord—good, it's intact . . . there's the heart—we see all four chambers . . . here's the stomach—let's measure the size—that's what we would expect at seventeen weeks; good . . . now let's see the head—let's take some measurements—oh, this is not so good—the head is very small—I'm so sorry, this baby has anencephaly."

Shock, fear, numbness, incredible sadness. In the space of a few seconds, our dreams for this baby were shattered. My husband and I cried and held each other, and on our way home, we stopped by the rectory at church to talk with our priest, who was also a close friend. I thought it was a strange question when he asked us if we wanted to have the baby christened in utero, but as I thought about it, I was really touched. My mind was swimming with a million thoughts, but I felt some comfort in knowing that regardless of what happened, our baby would be welcomed into heaven. We agreed to have it christened that Sunday. Russ and I called our good friends Dave and Wendy, who had agreed to be godparents just a couple of weeks earlier, to tell them of our decision.

When we got home the house was quiet—too quiet. I was cold and tired and just wanted to go to sleep and forget for a little while. Our children, Amy and Gregory, arrived home from school at four o'clock as usual. We sat them down and explained that the baby was not healthy and wouldn't live very long, if at all. Amy started crying, and Gregory's only comment was, "I'd rather me die than the new baby die." I couldn't believe how sensitive he was for a seven-year-old. I thought all of our hearts would break, and I remember thinking that if God were merciful, He wouldn't let me carry this baby to term.

On Saturday, we called Dr. Hermann at home to see if he knew the sex of the baby, because we had forgotten to ask about this during our visit. He said he was almost positive it was a girl. A baby girl. The name we had picked out was Gabrielle Vivian. Now I had a name for this little baby who was turning my world upside down for the second time. The first time had been when we found out I was pregnant—she was an unexpected blessing.

On Sunday morning, Dave and Wendy arrived with their two girls. There were lots of hugs and tears. It was an emotional day but one full of love and compassion. As the weeks and months after the christening went by, we all had our bouts with overwhelming sadness, anger, and anxiety about what the future held for us and the baby. Work was difficult; nursing is a physically and mentally demanding job, and some days I felt completely exhausted. But something was happening to me over the months of carrying this special child. I began to see my patients and their families in a different light. I became less judgmental, more compassionate, more willing to become involved in their lives on a personal and even spiritual level, more willing to listen to their problems. Everything took on new meaning. Why was baby Gabrielle having this powerful effect on my life?

Although Russ and I had always had a strong marriage, we became even closer during these months. Gabrielle forced us to examine some of our core beliefs, strengthened our commitment to each other, and helped us define how we would incorporate those beliefs into our lives. Could this little unborn child work such magic on the mother and father she would never know? Or did she somehow know us already?

The community around us was amazing. Total strangers were offering prayers for us and lending their support in many ways. Without knowing it, we had become a source of inspiration to many, simply because we had decided not to terminate the pregnancy. My thinking had changed completely: I had originally thought that a merciful God would take this baby early, but now I knew that a wise God was allowing me to keep her longer to bless the lives of others. My due date was approaching, and I prayed that I might be able to hold her for at least a few minutes; the doctors told us our time with her would be a matter of hours at most.

When our beautiful baby arrived on February 10, it was obvious that the hospital staff was prepared to help us deal with her death. But Gabby had other plans. We had arranged for a photographer to come to the hospital for the only family portrait Gabby would ever have. The photographer's studio was more than an hour away from the hospital, but she was there within an hour of the birth and took heavenly pictures of the baby with her parents and grandparents.

The next two days in the hospital were difficult. Gabby almost left us twice but ended up pulling through. She was fed through a tube and had to be kept in a warmer to regulate her temperature, but other than that, she was like a normal newborn. When Amy and Gregory came to see her they thought she looked like she was in a french fry machine—but they loved their little sister immediately. When I was ready to be discharged, it was clear that the nurses had no idea what to tell me regarding Gabby's care. Nobody had expected her to live this long. I was sent home with the standard postpartum instructions, a referral to a home hospice nurse, and lots of hugs, tears, and good wishes.

When we got home, we knew our time with Gabby would be limited, but we didn't want to turn our lives into a death watch. So everyone tried to return to their normal routines. I had so much help and support, with meals coming in, neighbors shuttling the kids around, friends coming to do laundry and errands—I felt truly blessed. We were able to take Gabby to Mass the following Sunday, and she was the object of the homily—on miracles and faith. I'll never forget how we felt when Father Bob asked Russ to hold her up for all to see. Her little life was affecting so many people in different ways, but mostly, everyone was in awe.

On Tuesday, Gabby's condition worsened, and by Thursday afternoon it was clear the end was near. I called Russ home from work and the kids home from school. After our priest came over and gave her the anointing of the sick she seemed more comfortable. Later in the evening, her breathing and heart rate became erratic. She was about to leave us. We all gathered around, and I held her as she breathed her last bit of life on earth. That was it. She was gone.

But was she really? More than a hundred people came to her memorial mass, and I received cards and letters and phone calls for weeks and weeks afterward. People told us how much her short life had affected theirs. Preachers gave sermons about the faith that surrounded her; neighbors told me they used Gabby as an example to their children of the value of life. Others told us that her story was a testament to them of the tenacity of the human spirit. This sweet child who should have lived only a few minutes fought to stay alive and preach her sermon for more than a week.

It has been three months now since Gabby died. But the miracle of her life still permeates every aspect of our lives and our thoughts. The children feel as though they have their own personal guardian angel who smiles down on them and even giggles with them from time to time. Just a few weeks ago, Gregory got a call from the Little League telling him what team he would play on this year. When they told him it was the Angels, we knew Gabby was up there, acting as a very influential member of the selection committee.

Gabby was a sunbeam . . . lent to us too briefly.

— Vivian Antrim
Menomonee Falls, Wisconsin

The Victory

ITH ONE PHONE call, a nightmare began that would span more than five years. A tender voice on the line informed me that our fifteen-year-old son was involved with drugs and alcohol and had been for quite some time. Shock gripped me.

We took our son, Taylor, to the county health department and had him tested for drug use. His drug levels broke their record for that substance. By the end of the week, we had admitted him to a local rehabilitation program. Six weeks later he was discharged and I thought the nightmare was over. But it was just beginning. Two months later he was arrested at school for sale and possession of marijuana. Months became years, and a pattern of drug abuse and arrests developed. In one year alone he was arrested ten times. Finally he was sentenced to six months in jail.

After visiting Taylor in jail each Sunday, my husband

and I would drive home and sit in front of our house and weep. How could this have happened? I prayed often for Taylor. When he was out of jail and living elsewhere, I invited him to dinner every Monday evening and to every family function.

I prayed that someone he respected would come into his life. The name of his former Boy Scout leader came to mind, a peace officer whom I saw soon after at a church function. I told him about Taylor and the impression I'd had. He said without hesitation that he would go and see him.

Two days later I was sitting at the sewing machine when, oddly enough, I saw in my mind the officer standing in a room embracing my son. Tears were flowing down both of their faces. I looked at the clock. It was 2:15 P.M. When the officer called later that evening, I told him I knew he had been to see Taylor around 2:15 that afternoon. He confirmed that he had gone where I could not go and be welcomed. My heart overflowed with gratitude.

From that time on, I felt infused with a powerful confidence and sense of peace. I realized that great blessings could result if I would continue to be faithful and diligent in my efforts to love and pray for my son.

One Monday morning I had a strong feeling that I should pray that my son be given a special dream, for it was only when he slept that he was still enough to listen. All the talking in the world over the past several years hadn't gotten through to him, so perhaps his subconscious mind would be more receptive. Even the words to say came gently to my mind. I was startled. I doubted that I had understood this spiritual nudging correctly. Could I do such a thing? However, the words came so strongly that I finally uttered them in my prayer. I was moved to ask specifically that my son have a bright recollection of all his guilt and feel the total responsibility of his actions, but also know immediately that his Heavenly Father loved him and would easily forgive him.

Time passed. Then late one summer night Taylor came to the house. He stood in the foyer, unsure of his welcome. When he said he had come to apologize for his behavior, I ran to him and threw my arms around him, and we both wept. For about two hours he described the pain of what he'd been going through and begged for our forgiveness.

My husband, who had been deeply hurt, was skeptical at first. But after talking long hours, I witnessed a second miracle that night as tears came to my husband's eyes and his heart was finally softened.

Some time later, as he continued to make his way back into the normal circles of our lives, Taylor was asked to speak at a leadership-training meeting at our church. As he stood and recounted his miraculous change of heart he said, "One night I had a dream, and in the dream I had a bright recollection of all my guilt. I felt the burden of all my actions but knew immediately that my Heavenly Father loved me and had forgiven me."

I was overcome with emotion. I knew then as never before that not only had my prayers been answered but that a wise and merciful God had graciously taught me what to pray for.

Eighteen months later my son was preparing to leave on a mission for our church. We are Mormons, and in our church, thousands of young men leave their homes each year to serve two-year missions in different parts of the world. To the casual observer, these are the boys riding around town on bicycles, dressed in white shirts, ties, and helmets, but few people really understand how much they sacrifice—and gain—in the process. We knew it would be a great experience for our son and were overjoyed he had made the decision to go.

At the church meeting where we bade farewell to our missionary sons and daughters before they left, there were nearly five hundred people in attendance for Taylor. Friends from Hawaii arrived, bringing with them a braided green lei, which they presented to him just before the meeting began. This particular lei, they explained, was one villagers placed on triumphant warriors when they returned victorious from battle. They encouraged him to wear it when he spoke to the congregation.

However, when Taylor stood to talk, he wasn't wearing the lei. I worried that our friends would be hurt. Then, near the end of his speech, he took out the lei and explained the tradition associated with it. He said that although he felt like a warrior going to battle for "good," there was someone else there who was the real warrior, someone who had waged a more difficult war and won. He then turned to me and reached for my hand, led me to his side, and lovingly placed the lei around my neck.

Many years before, I had heard it said that the only time we fail as parents is when we give up on our children. When Taylor placed the lei around my neck that day, as tears streamed down his face and mine, I realized the truth of that statement. Although it had been painful to stand back and watch him struggle, I had learned the hard lessons of acceptance and patience. But most of all, I came to understand the power of hope.

—JO ST. THOMAS
Las Vegas, Nevada

The Rose

M Y MOTHER WAS sick for twelve years. She did not waste away, eaten by despair and disease. She struggled courageously against the invader that reduced her body to a fragile vessel of weakness and pain. Her spirit burned through the ash and debris of her terminal illness until she herself—emaciated and trembling—resembled the stem of a rose.

It was not the first time she had lived on grit. But she had kept many secrets.

She went on living, ravaged by illness, aching in body but free in mind. Even when she was bedridden, her roots sought sustenance from the world—she turned outward toward her children and grandchildren. She consumed news, chatted with friends. She was not interested in her feeble body or in her aches and pains. She was interested in politics, sports, fashion, gardening, and her daughters. She loved my sister and me with a love that surpassed understanding.

Mom came of age beneath the blood-red Georgia sun. As a very young girl, she stooped from the burden of sharecropping. She was freckled from the sun beating down on the fields; she was often hungry and sometimes beaten. She had to be dirty sometimes—that was the most humiliating part of poverty. And no one taught her how to hug. She would take a deep breath and stiffen her elegant spine when her carefree children fell across her lap. She would exhale slowly as we encircled her shoulders with our youthful arms. She allowed us to touch her as if we were engaging in some strange tribal ritual—she understood that children needed hugs, even if she did not quite understand why. And she was determined that we would have the pretty dresses, savory food, and warm embraces that she had not received.

She never talked about her childhood—there was no place for her past in the fairy princess world she spun for her daughters. Telling them about her history of hunger and sorrow would have given them nightmares.

When I turned six, my birthday cake was festooned with sunset-pink roses from Mama's garden. The sharecropper's scrawny kid had become a lady in thick canvas gardening gloves. The roses she grew perfumed the air. Her house was spotless. She cooked huge meals for us. She filled our plates and never chided us with tales about what it was like to be hungry. Our baths spewed scent and bubbles, and we never heard the story of how she and her sister stole soap from a filling station in order to get clean. Our bedroom floors were littered with shoes, and we never imagined what it was like to have only one pair of tight and cracking hand-me-down oxfords.

Shopping with Mom was a celebration of dresses and skirts. She wanted us to have everything that "they were all wearing." I never knew who "they" were—looking back, I suspect "they" were the kids who teased a skinny little share-cropper's daughter who had only two dresses to her name. Mom would not discuss anything of the sort with her children. She protected us from the real and imagined monsters of her own past.

She tried to shelter us when we became middle-aged, too. But when both your parents die, it does not matter how old you are; you become an orphan.

Our father had nursed Mom for years before he became sick. No one expected her to outlive him. The morning he passed, I patted my mother's bird-boned shoulders. She shook with grief and rage. It was not supposed to be this way! She had planned to die before him.

She wanted to die.

But as she looked at her children, wounded by grief, she chose life for as long as she could cling to it. Outliving her prognosis, she sorted through pictures, old report cards, birthday notes, and clippings about school plays. Barely able to sit erect, she gathered my childhood into a box. There was the picture of me in a dress ruffled like a doll's, there was the summer reading certificate and my tiny pink glasses. The box held four decades of memories, from kindergarten to new motherhood to my son's high school graduation.

Before she died, she gave me my past—all of it sorted with love and dreams. My mother bequeathed me a past full of hugs and roses. In that collection, there is only one picture of my mother as a child. Her cheeks are thin. Her eyes are wary. Her hair is inexpertly chopped off. She looks as if she expects something unpleasant to happen.

My father had been gone a year and a half when Mom joined him. She shut her eyes and became one with the past that was my legacy.

In the blank pain that numbed the days after her death, I clawed her rosebush from her backyard. I knew the rosebush well—it had been years since Mom could tend to its needs. I carried the rosebush to my house and transplanted it into my backyard. I brought the past, my glorious childhood, and the sterling symbol of strength into my future.

Some women love with cautionary tales. Some try to enforce gratitude by drawing grim comparisons between their own deprivation and the gifts they give their children. Some people cannot give what they never got. My mother gave when she had nothing, when every breath was a battle. She loved with courageous silence. It was not from her that I learned of her deprived childhood. My mother loved by making the world a prettier place—full of roses and dreams.

When orphanhood overwhelms me and I feel the absence of that compelling love, all I need to do is look at Mom's roses. They have taken over my fence and are stretching toward the sun.

—DIANE GOLDBERG
Charlotte, North Carolina

In the Arms of Love

HE SWEET SMELL of peanut butter cookies filled my kitchen that cold day in January. The warmth of the oven was a contrast to the rainy winter storm raging outside my window. The sounds of children playing floated down the hall from their rooms. With three of them, our lives were filled with love and a constant flutter of activity. I had had difficulty getting pregnant, and so as each child came to our family, we felt very lucky. After having two healthy sons, we were finally given our precious daughter. Born the day after Christmas, she was a very welcome gift that year.

All morning the boys, Brian and Eric, had been chanting, "We want peanut butter cookies! We want peanut butter cookies!" I had promised them that just as soon as they cleaned their rooms, we would share our favorite treat together. But after a few minutes, I could tell by the sounds down the hall that there was more playing than cleaning going on. I walked down to the boys' room to encourage them to "get with it" and realized that our daughter, Amy, was not with them. Immediately my mind went to our back-yard. As I opened the back door, I caught sight of something in the Jacuzzi. Floating facedown in the water was my precious two-year-old daughter. I pulled her out of the cold water by the back of her little turquoise overalls and looked down into her face: it was white, cold, and lifeless.

I don't have the words to describe the pain I felt as I held this little darling in my arms. Running through the house I screamed, "Call 911. Hurry, Brian, your sister has drowned! Call 911!" I ran out the front door, carrying Amy's limp, wet body as I yelled for anyone to help. Through the bushes and into the neighbors' yard I ran, shouting, "Help me, please, somebody help me!" My neighbors, Dodie and Al, were seldom home during the day, but thank goodness they were there this day. Dodie took Amy from me and dropped her to the grass, instinctively administering mouth-to-mouth resuscitation as I helplessly watched and prayed for my daughter's life.

Soon friends and neighbors gathered around us. Dodie and Opal, another good friend, took turns doing CPR. Amy was still not breathing. My baby wasn't breathing! Within about twenty minutes the sheriff's department arrived and began CPR, but still no sign of life. I held Amy's hand as we rushed to the hospital while the sheriff tirelessly continued the CPR. The San Bernadino County Hospital was only a short distance away, and the minute we arrived, a team of doctors took Amy into the emergency room. Never had I prayed so hard, so sincerely.

Amy's heart had not been beating for over half an hour. I knew what that meant, and all those thoughts began to overwhelm me as I waited alone for my husband, Mark, to get to the hospital. After forty-five agonizing minutes the doctor told me that Amy's heart was beating again, but that a machine was doing the breathing for her.

Mark finally arrived at the hospital not knowing the severity of the situation. As he looked at his daughter in her desperate condition—tubes in her mouth, nose, arms, and a breathing machine giving her life—he was devastated. He immediately called a friend from our church and, along with Amy's uncle Doug, gave her a special blessing of healing, in accordance with the custom of our religion. As the beautiful words came forth, a sense of peace settled over us. We suddenly felt comfort in the knowledge that Amy was in God's hands—she was encircled in the arms of His love, and for the first time that day, we felt hope.

The chief neurologist at the hospital, Dr. Ashwal, came over to us and said, "I don't even know you, but I do know of your strong faith and family support. If I could just say one thing, it would be to hold on to that faith to help you get through this experience. If Amy makes it through the first seventy-two hours, there is a 98 percent chance she will live, but there will be brain damage to deal with. She'll be in the pediatric intensive care unit for three to four months, with a minimum cost of eighty thousand dollars, and then she'll be in basic care for an undetermined length of time." I was in shock. No matter which way we looked at it, the prognosis was grim.

Every measure was taken to save Amy's life. The staff worked on her constantly while she lay in a deep coma. The drugs, the tube placed through her tiny neck, a steel bolt inserted into her shaved head—all the finest medical technology was used in an effort to bring our child back. I felt immeasurable gratitude for this incredible team of doctors, but I still cried when they brought me Amy's beautiful blond curls in a small, brown paper bag.

During that first seventy-two hours, a special nurse had been assigned to us. At one point during the night, as she and I stood alone together in the intensive care unit, I pleaded with this woman to be completely honest with me. I needed to know the truth about Amy's prognosis; I needed to be prepared. She looked at me with hesitation but with great compassion as she spoke the words I was dreading: "I have worked with over a hundred drowning patients. Of all of them, no one with a pH level as low as 6.6 like Amy's has ever lived. Not one. A few with a pH of 6.8 have lived, but as vegetables. You may want to consider whether or not you want her life to continue in that manner."

So there it was. A truth shared in the darkness of the night between two women . . . two women who, in their own separate lives, had been profoundly touched and forever altered by the experience of loving and caring for a child . . . two mothers.

Amy looked so sweet and peaceful as she lay in the coma. It was comforting just to be in her presence. But I soon found out the impossibility of being content with just that as I began to envision a lifetime of such an inert existence. I ached to hear the sound of her small voice when I would ask her, "Are you Mama's baby?" to which she would tease, "No! Da-da's baby!" We would play this little game over and over, and every time she would squeal with delight.

Our little fighter made it through those critical seventy-two hours. Dr. Ashwal met us early the next morning. He wanted to try to take her out of her coma, but there were many risks. We could lose her altogether, but the alternative of leaving her in a coma seemed like a cruel sentence. The doctor explained that if he attempted this procedure, we probably wouldn't see any movement or eye function for several days. It would be a long, slow process, and we needed to be patient.

Mark and I stood on either side of Amy's bed as the tubes were removed. Around noon she was taken off the drugs that had kept her in the coma and had kept her alive. Again, the doctor warned us that it would be many days, if at all, before we might notice any change in Amy. Yet there we stood—waiting, hoping.

In not more than an hour, Amy's eyes suddenly opened. She looked up at me and said the most beautiful words I had ever heard: "Mama, Mama, Mama." In disbelief, Mark called her name and she turned to him and said, "Da-da," and then closed her eyes once again.

Amy's nurse was in the room with us. Breathlessly, she exclaimed, "I can't believe it! This is incredible!" At that moment, we all knew that God had given us a miracle.

Amy left the pediatric intensive care unit the next day, not even one full week after her accident. All of us around her who had been prepared to endure three or four months of painful, anxious waiting agreed as the doctor proclaimed, "What a miracle. We attribute this to a power greater than us all."

Fifteen years later, Amy is still a miracle and a blessing to our family. As I look at her amazing life now, I sometimes think about where Amy might have gone during those first few lifeless moments after the drowning. Could she have spoken to God? And if so, might they have discussed whether it was time for her to go home to Him or whether there was still work to do and people's lives to touch here on earth? I don't know the answers to those questions, but I somehow know that during those few precious moments, He must have tenderly picked her up and, cradling her in the arms of His love, brought her back to us.

— DEBBIE RHODES
Loomis, California

A Mother's Spirit

'M A COP. I'm a sheriff with the El Dorado County Sheriff's Department in Northern California. We work out of a small gold rush–era town called Placerville. I've been with the sheriff's department for six years now, but I'd like to tell you about something that happened pretty early in my career. It started with a missing persons report.

In the state of California, there are upward of sixty-four missing persons reports filed every year. Most of these reports turn out to be kids who took off from their families for a while, spouses who take a short vacation from their marriages, or even folks trying to shake an old friendship. On the evening of June 10, 1994, I was assigned to a missing persons report that had been filed the day before. I have the completed report here on my desk right now. It is a short document—only three typed pages of cop talk about the incident.

What this small document leaves out is a miracle, a miracle that could never be translated into a police report and filed away in a drawer. This is the story of a woman named Christene Dawn Skubish and her three-year-old son, Nicky.

Christene Skubish and her son, Nicky, were headed up Highway 50 toward the Nevada town of Carson City. Some of you may know Highway 50. It is one of the two major routes through the Sierra Nevada mountains to Lake Tahoe. It is a beautiful road, but one with many dangers. Slow and winding in parts, fast and narrow in others, this heavily forested road has been the scene of many an accident. Christene left for Carson City on a Sunday night and hadn't been heard of since. The following Thursday, both her family in California and her friend in Nevada filed missing persons reports on the young mother and her son. Our department put together a flyer with her picture and description, and we went to work.

I worked the graveyard shift that Friday, from 10 P.M. until 8 A.M. One of my jobs that night was trying to find any sign that Christene might have come through Placerville on Sunday. I began by canvassing the all-night gas stations. By 5 A.M., I'd found a clerk who remembered that a girl who looked like Christene had stopped at the station late one night. She'd bought gas and had mentioned that she was headed to Carson City. She looked tired, the clerk remembered.

An odd call had come into our department earlier that morning, about 3 A.M. It was from a woman, calling from a pay phone on the side of the road on Highway 50. In a voice shaking with emotion, she described what she had just seen on the shoulder of the highway—the dead, naked body of a woman. A white woman with brown hair. Two different patrol units had met this caller, and she had led them back to the scene. But there was nothing there. No body, no sign that there had ever been one. The officers used all of their searchlights, flashlights, and spotlights but could see nothing in the darkness of the forest.

But something about the description of the woman's body struck a chord with me. It sounded just like Christene Skubish. I decided to check it out myself when the sun came up. Perhaps I would be able to see something in the daylight that the other officers had missed. I was also anxious to check it out because I had just learned that members of Christene's family had arrived in Placerville. They'd driven all night from Southern California, vowing to search the seventy-two miles between Placerville and Carson City themselves. If there was a body out there—or even worse, two bodies—I didn't want them to be the ones to discover it.

That early in the morning there was little traffic on the highway. I was able to drive slowly along in my cruiser, checking all the while for anything that looked out of place, any sign that an accident had occurred. At 6 A.M. I saw it— a child's shoe by the side of the road. I pulled my car over to the side as best I could; it was a narrow spot on the road without much of a shoulder. At the edge of the shoulder the hill fell steeply into a wooded canyon. And looking down into the canyon I could see it—a red compact car, California license 2XBY018. Christene Skubish's car.

The hill was so steep that I didn't really walk down to the car, I slid down to it. I stopped myself by sliding into the back of the heavily damaged car and made my way around to the driver's side. Looking into the window I could see Christene, dead. She was still strapped into the driver's seat, slumped over the steering wheel. There were severe lacerations, but there was no real blood on her face. Reaching into the car, I confirmed the fact that she was dead. I looked across to the passenger side, and there was her son, Nicky, beside her. He lay sideways on the seat with his back to me, curled into a fetal position, clad only in his underwear. From where I stood, he appeared to be dead, too. I had found both missing persons. Climbing back up the steep hill to my car I radioed the dispatcher—"Two decedents. I need the coroner and some backup for traffic control."

Then I slid back down the hill again, this time to approach from Nicky's side. I rolled him over and shone a light in his eyes. No reaction from his pupils. I felt for a pulse on his neck. Nothing. Then I saw his chest move. After five days in a wrecked car, this little boy was still alive! I shouted his name, trying to get him to respond to me. No response. He was alive but near death from dehydration.

Nicky made it. He was in intensive care for two and a half weeks, but he made it. The doctors said that his condition was so grave that had I not found him when I did, he would not have lived for another hour.

So what had happened out there on Highway 50 that night? How did I find the one spot in seventy-two miles on a dark, lonely mountain road where Christene's wrecked car was hidden? Who was the dead woman on the side of the road? Christene died instantly, still tightly held by her safety belt. But Debra Hoyt, the woman who phoned in the report of the woman on the side of the road, knows what she saw— Christene Skubish. When she was shown a photo of Christene, she said yes, that was the woman she had seen lying there. Debra believes that she was given a vision by God, that she was used by God to summon help for the still-living Nicky. Many people in our area believe that Debra saw the spirit of Christene, desperately trying to save her son. Christene's mother, Brenda, believes that God was watching over Nicky those five days he was in the crashed car. "He's the one that saved Nicky. If it hadn't been for God's hand on Nicky and Nicky's love and devotion for his mother and his mother's love and devotion for him . . ."

What do I believe? Like I said, I'm a cop. I didn't go into this job with any starry-eyed notion that I could save the world. I knew that I would spend a lot of time with the bad side of humanity, not the good side. But I remember what I said in my job interview, just a little over a year before I found little Nicky still alive in that car: if sometime during my career I could affect someone's life in a positive way, that would fulfill my career goals. And I did.

I'm a cop, but I believe in miracles. As ordinary people, we might not always understand miracles completely when they happen to us, but there are a couple of things I *do* know since that day. One is that God had His hand in what happened out there on Highway 50. And the other is that a mother's love and desire to save her child must be a pretty powerful thing. But facts like those don't always get told—at least, not in an official police report.

— RICH STRASSER
Auburn, California

Worth Waiting For

I SAT IN MY car in the parking lot of the doctor's office, my head resting on the steering wheel, sobbing. *Why can't I get pregnant? Why can't I give my husband the one thing we both want so badly?!* I was young, I was healthy—what was the matter with my body? At times like this, your mind does crazy things, wandering back to everything you've ever done wrong and you think, *Am I being punished?* I even entertained the crazy thought that if I didn't get pregnant soon, Peter, my husband, would leave me and find a woman who could bear his child.

But that cruel thought never entered my husband's mind. He stuck by me through every examination, every test, every fertility treatment, every insurance nightmare. A warm, caring, loving, and funny man, he is also a very wise man. And after listening to my sobs one night he said, "Cathy, raising children is about parenting, not about giving birth. Why don't we look into adoption?"

Peter was the catalyst in our adoption odyssey. I was still convinced that I would someday get pregnant, but Peter steered me toward other options. We made an appointment with an adoption attorney. After our first talk with her, once again I burst into tears in our car, realizing that this meant we were closing the door on fertility treatments. But Peter was strong. He calmed me down, and we talked about what we'd learned from the attorney. By the time we arrived home that day, I was ready to begin work on our first step toward adopting a child—putting together the photo album that prospective moms would view.

After only three months we heard from our attorney—a mother had chosen us! We were elated and peppered the attorney with questions. "Who is she? When can we meet her?" A meeting was set for the following week, and I was so excited I could hardly sleep at night. The baby was due in six weeks, and if the birth mother liked us and we liked her, we could have a baby in just six weeks! What an incredible thought!

For the next six weeks we spent quite a bit of time with the birth mother and her boyfriend, the birth father. They stayed with us for the weekend, and we took them out to lunches and dinners. I bought her some maternity clothes and paid her rent and some past due bills. Things seemed to be going great, and I started decorating the baby's room. My friends and family were as excited as we were—they even had a baby shower for us.

The birth happened right on schedule. I received a phone call from her boyfriend on the due date, telling me that she had gone into labor. I called Peter, and within minutes we were on our way to the hospital. Amidst tears of joy, we arrived in time for the delivery of a beautiful six-pound, eleven-ounce baby girl. The delivery nurse rushed the baby by us on her way do basic tests and clean her up; we were only able to see our new baby girl from behind the window in the maternity ward. Wanting to share our joy, we went to see the birth mother, but tired and in need of rest, she didn't want to see us. It seemed like a normal response, so we weren't concerned.

But over the next two weeks her behavior became increasingly unpredictable. She announced that she wanted to take the baby home with her from the hospital "just for the weekend," to say good-bye. Peter and I went home empty-handed and confused, wondering if the adoption was really going to happen after all. After the weekend, she phoned us and told us she was ready to give the baby to us. We leapt into the car to go and pick up our precious bundle. All was not yet settled, however.

We received several tearful phone calls from her after we took the baby home. On the third day, it was her boyfriend who called. His message was unbelievable—if we didn't return the baby to them within two hours we would be reported to the police as kidnappers! Heartbroken, we brought our baby girl back to her birth parents. Since the adoption papers had not yet been signed, we had no rights. This same cycle was repeated several times—come and get her—no, bring her back! We actually got as far as a meeting with the birth parents to sign the papers. As it happened, though, our attorney had neglected to obtain one last critical piece of necessary paperwork. The birth parents took this as a sign that they were meant to keep their baby and once again asked to have her back. And then they called another time. We finally asked them never to contact us again.

It was an incredibly painful time for us. Peter and I kept to ourselves for the next several weeks. Most agonizing of all was the fact that many of our friends, unaware of the situation, kept calling to congratulate us on our new baby. After one month of hibernation, we finally ventured out to a fund-raising dinner that Peter's company was involved with. It was refreshing to sit at a table of ten people, all clients and their spouses, without anyone knowing about our traumatic situation. By the end of the evening, the wives were talking about children. When someone asked whether we had children, I was able for the first time to tell our story without crying. I finally felt at peace with what had happened.

Summer had arrived, and Peter and I made plans for a much-needed vacation. We planned to spend a full week in the mountain air of the Sierras at Lake Tahoe. Just the thing to renew our hopes for a family. June 30, the day we were leaving, was a lazy one. We didn't feel the need to get up and hit the road right away but rather were still lying lazily in bed with the newspaper and steaming cups of coffee when the phone rang.

Peter finished the conversation and hung up the phone. Turning to me with a wide grin on his face, he said, "Remember my client Ted? You met him and his wife, Kelly, at the fund-raiser a few weeks ago." I nodded, "Of course I remember them." I said. "Well, his wife is down in Texas right now, and a good friend of hers just had a baby two hours ago. A baby that she wants to give up for adoption! They want to know if we are interested." Were we ever!

Instead of heading for Lake Tahoe as planned, we found ourselves a short twelve hours later in Texas. The next morning we met our little girl. Words cannot describe how Peter and I felt when we first held her. We spent the next few days in Texas taking care of legal matters and arrived home on July 3 with a newborn baby daughter. Next month our daughter, Mary Jo, will be two years old, and I can honestly say that the last two years of our lives have been the happiest ever.

When I first sat down to begin composing this miracle tale, Peter and I had begun the search for a second child to adopt. Through our longing and our waiting, we have developed patience—a quality I know we will need in raising *two* precious daughters. For just last night we learned that we are once again to be blessed with a child—a birth mother has chosen us to be the parents of her baby girl, due this fall.

—CATHY LONSDALE
Sacramento, California

The Good Custodian

WE ARE TOLD that angels appear as voices, dreams, or visions. They carry messages of hope. Of course, some people insist that angels don't exist. Other people ask why they appear only to certain humans, though still others say that angels come to everyone. In any case, I suppose the question to ask is: who will recognize them when they come?

My son, Stevie, was living in San Francisco and had been HIV positive for ten years. In June 1995 he came down with a sinus infection and was in and out of the hospital three times that month, but somehow he found the strength to make it to the opening night of his play. He had been producing a play in Morelia, Mexico, and it was so well received that he was asked to put it on in the barrios of Northern California. He begged the hospital to allow him to go to opening night. An ambulance, IV, and walking cane were arranged for opening night. As the play ended, Stevie went onto the stage and was able to say only a few words. "If my play is successful and one person learns about HIV and AIDS, then my life has been a success."

My husband and I traveled from Ohio to visit Stevie for Thanksgiving, but during our visit he became violently ill, and we called the rest of the family to fly to California because it was apparent that Stevie's death was imminent. He continued to get worse, and he suffered terribly during his days in the hospital. We were there as a family to love and support him, and he was surrounded by his sisters and cousins, but the few days we expected him to survive turned into three long, painful weeks for all of us. We are a very religious Hispanic family, normally full of faith and hope, but watching Stevie's agony those weeks shook us to the very core.

After his nineteenth day in the hospital, the doctors told us they thought he had a lesion on his brain, and if they could confirm that with an MRI, they could operate and perhaps improve his condition. At that point, Stevie couldn't talk, eat, or move, but by motioning to certain letters on an alphabet board my daughter Ginny had created, he let us know how much he hated the idea of having the MRI. Ginny and I were at his side as they wheeled him in for the procedure, and when they told Ginny she had to leave, she saw the tears running down his face. He was so vulnerable, so afraid.

As my daughter and I sat in the waiting room, I realized that our collective spirit had hit bottom. It was our lowest moment. There was so little hope, and yet we would have to make the decision whether they should operate or not, after learning the results of the brain scan. Stevie had requested that no extreme measures be taken to prolong his life, and we felt the weight of that request and all its implications. As we sat together, we seemed to be enveloped in a thick cloud of despair. My husband had decided to continue to pray the rosary in the waiting room, as he had for the last nineteen days.

During our weeks at the hospital, my family had come to know many of the nurses and other hospital workers. This particular afternoon, a friendly custodian was mopping the floor in the area of the waiting room. He was an older, kindly looking African-American who seemed to take genuine pleasure in his mundane tasks. His name tag simply said RON. As he approached us and noticed our long faces, he cheerfully commented, "Hello, ladies. . . . How're you doing? . . . You here for an MRI? . . . Your son, ma'am? . . . Your brother, miss? . . . How long's he been in the hospital?"

In our state of deep sadness we almost ignored him—or tried to, at least. None of us was in any mood to make idle talk with a stranger, and we were a little put off by his amiable nature. Couldn't he see our suffering? Didn't he realize we wanted to be left alone? When we curtly offered a few halfhearted answers to his questions, he continued to mop the floor but began to share some thoughtful, spiritual counsel about having faith and hope in coping with our situation. He admonished us to continue praying for strength, and to be courageous in accepting God's will. We were reminded that all things are in His hands, that there was a purpose for everything, and that our prayers should always reflect the attitude of "thy will be done." There was a gentleness about Ron, but also a sense of certainty in the words he offered. It was almost more certainty than we could bear at the moment—I found myself wondering where the goodness of "his" God was now, in my family's hour of need.

Ron finally decided to leave us to our thoughts and move on to another area, but as he walked away, a strange thing happened. An almost tangible feeling of peace swept over us just as he departed. A warm serenity filled the air and gave renewed strength to our disheartened spirits—and it surprised all of us.

On December 19, the doctors ended up operating on Stevie, but he passed away on December 22, five days before his fortieth birthday. In his short life he had taught many about the real meaning of love.

As we prepared to leave the hospital and were saying goodbye to all the staff members who had carried us through our ordeal, we looked for the good custodian, Ron. We wanted to thank him for his encouragement and friendship. But no one seemed to know where we could find him. As a matter of fact, no one even knew anyone by that name on the custodial staff. We asked everyone if they knew Ron—the nurses, the other maintenance workers, the supervisors, the doctors—and they all said they didn't. We talked to the hospital cashier, who told us she had worked at the hospital for fifteen years. She had never heard of the man we were searching for, or of any employee named Ron.

As any mother might imagine, there was much grief in my heart over the loss of my son. But my family's unusual encounter with the man called Ron let our hearts believe something almost too wondrous to fully comprehend. We knew this much, though—the good custodian had come for just a few moments to lift one family's spirits, to give them hope, and to make them less afraid—and for that we are grateful.

—MARIA GUADALUPE LOPEZ
Fostoria, Ohio

Legacy of Love

I T WAS THE most heartbreaking yet memorable Christmas Eve I and the thousand other people in attendance had ever experienced. It was the military funeral of "Captain" David Karl Clayson. Two rows of top navy brass in white crisp full-dress uniform sat at attention in the chapel that brisk afternoon in 1985, saying good-bye—with full military honors—to their friend and colleague.

But Captain Clayson was only eleven years old. He was my little prince, my son.

Everyone who knew him said he showed such great love and had a warmth that made everyone feel they were his friend. He was an absolute joy to our family for the eleven years he was with us. David was an unusually active, healthy boy who played baseball and soccer, excelled in every aspect of schoolwork, played the violin beautifully, and sang in a local children's chorus. He was never sick until that sudden headache at his violin teacher's house one afternoon.

It was just before Christmas 1984. My husband, Karl, a noted vascular surgeon, stood in the hospital emergency room holding our son's X rays in his hand. He was stunned. The pictures highlighted a growth on David's brainstem, and Karl's training forced him to acknowledge that it was only a matter of time before our David would be gone.

Karl and I and our daughters, Janie and Hannah, were in shock at the prognosis. Our whole world was turned upside down. But through it all, I was determined to make David's passage, if possible, a little bit more comprehendible. He was such an incredibly brave boy, an example to everyone.

I believed strongly in the certainty of life after death, as did our whole family. As each day passed, all I could think about was wishing there was a way to introduce David to my father, the grandfather he had never known, who surely would be waiting to welcome him in the next life. If only David could love and trust him as I had, and know that he would be waiting eagerly to greet him.

As a start, I placed a picture of my father, Lieutenant Commander E. Wayne Stratford, M.D., in his formal navy choker whites, on the table by David's bed, and spent hours telling him stories of his grandfather's heroic accomplishments during the Iwo Jima invasion and on board the U.S.S. *Lubbock*. In my heart, though, I was afraid that the picture and the stories wouldn't be enough.

Within just a day of the diagnosis, David's balance was gone. I held him up as he attempted an unsteady course down the hallway. By June he was using a wheelchair and had difficulty speaking. He moved his eyes—up and down for yes and from side to side for no.

I can't describe the pain of having to accept that the son I loved and adored was approaching the end of his life. I turned him in bed every hour of the day and night to avoid bedsores, and lifted his wheelchair into our car to give him as many outings as possible. There was nothing I wouldn't do for him—I took him everywhere. We went to the circus, to musicals, to amusement parks. I hired concert pianists, magicians, and clowns to fill the extra hours and to entertain his keen mind.

But the gift I wanted most desperately for David, and the one I prayed for the hardest, was to ease his passage by somehow helping him to know and to love the remarkable man he would soon join in death. How could I pass to him that priceless gift of love? I had no specific plan in mind. I had no idea where to turn. But I knew that it was what needed to be done, and I knew I'd need help doing it.

I learned later that a friend of ours, Richard Stoeltzing, couldn't get David out of his mind. We weren't close friends, but one Saturday afternoon, Dick knocked on our front door with an offer of help.

He had been driving home from an out-of-town business meeting where he'd sat in on a stirring appeal from the founder of Make-A-Wish, a children's aid organization. The speaker had challenged every sales representative present to go home and make a dying child's last few days a little easier.

Dick was moved by the challenge. He liked children, and he knew that they are excited by ships. In his position as commander with the naval reserve, he was scheduled for a formal change-of-command ceremony the following Saturday at the Alameda, California, Naval Air Station. One of the largest nuclear-powered aircraft carriers in the world, the U.S.S. *Carl Vinson*, was docked at Alameda. The ship carried five thousand men and a hundred airplanes. Dick's plan began to take shape.

There were built-in problems, he knew. David's health was failing. Dick thought we might not consider David up to the excursion. Even more doubtful, Dick also wondered if he carried enough clout to arrange for permission to take our son aboard.

He had one week to pull his plans together. He started by coming to talk to me. Unfortunately, when he put in a call to the public affairs officer on the U.S.S. *Carl Vinson*, the answer was no.

"Absolutely not! We're ready for sea drills, and nobody comes aboard before a drill. Besides, the crew has been promised shore leave for next weekend."

But Dick is a born salesman and he wouldn't give up that easily. "Hey, aren't there strings to pull? This is one special young man." He related David's grandfather's great contribution to the navy and the world as the first doctor ever to culture penicillin and inoculate bandages with it to save the lives of young marines dying of infections. The Bandage Brigade who raised the American flag over Iwo Jima came from Dr. Stratford's ship. That conversation put in motion the miracle for which I had been so earnestly praying. The navy had a debt of gratitude to repay.

As it happened, for the first time in twenty years Commander Stoeltzing received orders to wear his choker whites on Saturday, along with all the other military men in the ceremony. They looked exactly like my father in the picture by David's bed.

Coincidence? Maybe. But suddenly, as David gazed intently at the sea of hundreds of living, breathing men in white, I believe David's grandfather became more than just a picture. He began to come alive. We were piped on board as visiting dignitaries. The admiral and captain shook hands with us and personally welcomed us aboard. Later that afternoon, dozens of officers and staff members on the *Vinson* voluntarily stayed on board to give David a day none of them would ever forget. The wheelchair was set aside, and my husband carried David on his back.

Officers gave up precious shore leave to escort our party from deck to deck. Cameramen stayed on ship to videotape the activities so that David would have a memento.

Two ship chefs baked a special chocolate cake and decorated it with: To David Clayson, Honorary Member, U.S.S. *Carl Vinson*. It was a day of unbelievable compassion from men who had been trained for war. They didn't suspect that they were also fulfilling a mother's deepest prayers.

From that day on they were all friends and shipmates, and David was "Captain" David Clayson. Dick hung the captain's bell by our front door, to be sounded when the "captain" entered or left the house. As long as one arm could move, David solemnly saluted when Commander Stoeltzing came to call. David's bedroom was decorated like a bunk on board ship. Someone gave him a navy blanket to cover his bed. And the men on the *Vinson* didn't forget David. They regularly sent autographed photographs, came to see him in

Sacramento, and gave him their own navy stripes and a boson pin to remind him of the day their paths had crossed.

Military men were not alone in their devotion to David. A friend from church arranged with a local theater for a private showing of the movie *E.T.*, just released at that time. She wanted him to absorb the gentle message of E.T.'s longing to go home. The theater management invited forty of David's friends to join him and furnished free popcorn and drinks. So many wonderful things were done for David by a whole community.

David lived longer than the doctors ever expected. The next Christmas we had presents wrapped under the tree for him as he cheerfully encouraged everyone around him to live life to the fullest and to believe he would survive. But David never opened those presents. He slipped away on December 21, 1985, and his farewell was held on Christmas Eve. Janie, Hannah, and I played our violins as three-fourths of our family quartet, while David's smaller violin rested quietly on a music stand by our side. Our young son had packed a lot of living into his final few months. But most of all, our prayers for his peace had been miraculously answered.

David had gone confidently to meet the grandfather he already loved.

David—like E.T.—had gone home.

—JANE STRATFORD CLAYSON
Sacramento, California

And This Shall Be a Sign

I T WAS AN ordinary evening at home. My husband and I were watching television in our living room, and our children, Shane and Britny, were fast asleep. It was a part of day that I always looked forward to, the chance to spend some quiet time with my husband, R.J. He would settle into his favorite couch, and I would sit next to him in my rocking chair. That old curved oak rocking chair is my favorite piece of furniture in the whole house. It was where I sat to rock my two babies night after night when they were tiny. Such wonderful memories have been worn into that smooth wood.

Not long after we'd settled in that evening to watch our favorite programs, a commercial came on the screen. You know the type. Who knows what they are selling—it could be tires, insurance, or even fast food. The point is, they use cute little babies to sell it. I sat there in my rocking chair watching those tiny sweet faces and dimpled short legs, thinking about how much I'd enjoyed Shane and Britny when they were that age. And all of a sudden an intense longing came over me. I looked at my husband with wide, misty eyes, and he looked back at me with alarm.

"What? Oh, no, you're not thinking about . . . we should have done it years ago if that was what you wanted! Tell me you don't want another baby!" His arguments were valid—our son, Shane, was now three and a half, and our daughter was seven. Our lives had settled into a comfortable routine. Did we really want to start all over again with diapers and late-night feedings and all of the other things that come along with a newborn? Yes, I did want to start all over again. Yes, I did want to sit in that chair with a warm bundle sleeping in my arms. But R.J. was unconvinced.

"All right then, here's what I'll do. I'll pray for a sign, a sign that we should have a third child!" My sudden announcement surprised me. Sure, I believe in God. Sure, we go to church. But to pray for an answer to a question? Now there was something new for me! And just as surprising, R.J. agreed.

That night I prayed, asking God to please send me some kind of sign if we were meant to try for a third baby. God didn't have an answer for me that night. Or the next night, or the next. After a few days had passed, R.J. asked if I'd received my sign. "Not yet," I said, "but I'm still waiting."

Four days after we'd had that late-night baby discussion and after I'd begun to ask for a sign from the heavens, I was working alone in the corner of our bedroom where we keep our computer. There were a few E-mail addresses that I wanted to make note of, so I began to rummage around for a scrap of paper. I grabbed the first blank-looking piece I could find, an unfamiliar sheet of stationery, folded in half. After jotting the addresses on one side of the paper, I decided to copy even more information. I'd filled the first side, and so I unfolded the paper. "Hmm . . . what's this?" I said to myself as I noticed a small design of some sort in the corner. It was hard to identify, as I was holding it upside down. I turned the stationery right side up to take a closer look. What I then saw caused my heart to beat quickly—it was a tiny manger scene, with a line of scripture written underneath. "And this shall be a sign unto you; Ye shall find the babe wrapped in swaddling clothes, lying in a manger."

My sign! I'd received my sign! What else could explain this piece of paper? I'd never seen this paper before, nor had I ever had any stationery like it. I called R.J., my hand shaking as I dialed the phone. "I got our sign, honey. The answer is yes!"

"Now just calm down, Melinda. You've got babies on your mind, so of course you found a sign that confirmed what you wanted anyway."

I was crushed by R.J.'s response. How could he not believe that what had happened was truly a sign? I'd prayed and gotten a sign—did he need one, too?

"Yes, I think I do. I think I'd like to receive a sign about this, too," he said. "But don't you go calling everybody about this, now. We're just talking about it privately."

Well, I didn't call everybody, but I did pick up the phone and call my mother-in-law in Oregon. R.J.'s mother is my close friend, and we share quite a bit with each other about what happens in our lives. So I told her everything—about the commercial, about asking for a sign, about the sign I received, and about how her son now wanted a sign of his own!

"Honey, I think you'd better sit down," my mother-in-law said after I finished my tale. "I think I have the sign that R.J. is looking for." She went on to tell me about an experience she'd had just a few nights earlier. For many years, she and her cousin Lynne (who is also her best friend) had gotten together to pray. They would spend quiet time together a few evenings a week, praying for the health and safety of all of the members of their families. The children, their spouses, everyone was included. But the other night, in the midst of their prayers, Lynne had suddenly stopped and asked her, "Are Melinda and R.J. having another baby? I feel like God is nudging me to pray for the new life in Melinda!"

Another sign! What more could R.J. want?

Nothing, as it turned out, and we conceived on our first try! Our little baby, Kailee Marie, was born on January 25, 1997, and I can't imagine life without her!

— MELINDA EHLERS
Annapolis, Maryland

Prayers for Elijah

HREE HOURS AFTER giving birth at home to
our newborn son, Elijah, I momentarily
parted with my sweet baby boy and hobbled down the hallway to my home office. Exhausted and sore from the workout
of my life, I mustered the strength to turn on my computer,
log on to the Internet, and send an E-mail message announc-
ing Elijah's birth to a group of 1,500 people who subscribe to
my online newsletter.

To casual observers, I might have looked like another
pathetically addicted E-mail junkie, a business owner with
priorities so out of whack she couldn't even tear herself away
from her home office just hours after giving birth to her child.
But they would be wrong.

So why did I even have the desire to share the news of Elijah's birth with my newsletter subscribers? After all, most of
them are strangers to me, E-mail addresses from around the

world who receive a free online newsletter every two weeks. Writing the newsletter is just one of many tasks in my business. How did this list of strangers, business associates, and acquaintances make it to the "A" list—those who heard about Elijah's birth right after calls to our family and close friends? Let me tell you how it happened.

In my third month of pregnancy, my water broke and I almost miscarried Elijah. I was ordered to take complete bed rest and warned that I would probably lose the pregnancy. Before retiring to bed, in tears, I sent an E-mail message to my newsletter subscribers explaining the circumstances and asking for prayers from those who believed that prayer would make a difference. Then I went to bed and hoped for the best. Over the next two days, I was inundated with hundreds of prayers, E-mailed to me from newsletter subscribers of all faiths, in countries all over the world. My subscribers in turn sent my request for help to their pastors, rabbis, family members, and prayer groups, resulting in thousands of prayers for Elijah and me within a twenty-four-hour period.

Prayers of all kinds were sent my way. Some quoted scripture—"When you pass through the waters, I will be with you" (Isaiah 43:2); and some wove beautiful images for me to focus on—"You and your baby and family are wrapped in love and light." There were prayers from parents who knew what it was like to pray for the life of a child, and prayers from children themselves. This came from a ten-year-old: "Please Lord, help this little baby that Mommy's friend is having and take care of the baby so that we have a new child to love." And one dear soul in Romania wrote, "I don't pray to God too often, but I will pray for you."

Most of the subscribers who responded were strangers to me. We don't normally discuss faith issues in this newsletter—it is, after all, a business newsletter. But I knew that many on the list were devoted and compassionate people, since the focus of the newsletter was taking care of your marriage and family while growing your business. I took a chance by lifting the normal boundaries between business and home and requested help of a personal nature. The result was, I believe, miraculous.

Two days after being flooded with prayers, a neighbor drove me to the doctor's office for my follow-up ultrasound. I held her hand and cried, expecting to hear the worst. Instead, the ultrasound technician was puzzled—he could find nothing wrong. The next day my husband and I visited my medical doctor, who declared me entirely normal. He had no medical explanation for my miraculous recovery. Elijah and I were out of danger, and the pregnancy continued without incident. I will always believe that the thousands of online prayers I received were instrumental in saving Elijah's life.

So when I felt compelled to get the word out to my subscribers only hours after delivering Elijah, it wasn't that I couldn't keep my mind off of my work. It was because these people were now like family to me. I felt as though Elijah had hundreds of aunts and uncles in places as far away as Colombia and Iceland, who loved and cared about him and would celebrate with us his healthy arrival in the world.

— AZRIELA JAFFE
Lancaster, Pennsylvania

The Kindness of Strangers

ROM THE TIME my son was a little boy, he sent a valentine to the same woman every year. Let me tell you about that woman.

Thinking back sixty-three years ago, I can still feel the despair and helplessness that overwhelmed me as I stood in the hospital corridor, looking at my tiny son through a thick glass observation window. As I watched his chest rise and fall with each breath, I trembled with fear, knowing that if he was to live, I would need a miracle. The nurses had given me the clothes he'd been wearing when we brought him in; I clutched them tightly against my tear-stained face, breathing in his familiar scent and praying that somehow the intensity of my love would protect him from dying.

It was a wet, foggy winter in 1934. My husband and I were busy raising our two young children—Joanie, our two-year-old daughter, and Rudy Junior, our seven-month-old son. My husband, Rudy, was a traffic policeman at Fifth and Mission in San Francisco and was soon promoted to the Bureau of Inspection. It was a wild and woolly time to be a policeman in San Francisco, and he treasured the time he spent at home with his small family, far away from the long days immersed in the city's crime sprees. But even he couldn't keep his children safe from one of life's gravest dangers at that time—scarlet fever.

It took us by surprise, like a sudden rainstorm on a spring day. My daughter, Joanie, contracted this dreaded disease first—thankfully, her strong body was able to battle the sickness. We felt so blessed to have her life spared; so many young children died of scarlet fever in those days. Our family doctor had advised us to take our baby son, Rudy, to his grandmother's house in order to minimize the risk of his getting the disease, too. It was hard to leave him there. Even at such a young age he had boundless affection and charisma. His squeals of laughter and happiness could always put the sunshine back in our souls on even the foggiest San Francisco day.

Not long after his arrival at his grandmother's house, however, she called to tell us that he had a troublesome sore throat. In fact, he had a strep infection so severe that large abscesses began to grow in his throat. Frightened by this turn of events, we rushed him to San Francisco's Children's Hospital.

At the hospital, the doctor reluctantly informed us that, in many cases, scarlet fever is preceded by a strep infection, caused by a specific type of strep germ that manufactures a scarlet fever toxin. Not all strep infections cause scarlet fever, because not everyone is susceptible to the rash-producing toxin. With Rudy's high fever and enlarged lymph glands, the doctor insisted on operating right away to remove the abscesses; otherwise he thought our infant son would live only for a few more hours. With a voice empty of hope, he also informed us that if Rudy were to survive his strep infection and fight off the possibility of scarlet fever, he would need the blood serum of an adult who had survived scarlet fever within the last two to three months.

Because of his severe condition, the doctors placed my dying son alone in a small room behind an isolation window. It was agony not being able to hold him, to comfort him with our love through touching and cuddling. My husband and I could only stand in the hallway and look through the window, watching our son's lonely struggle from behind thick glass. Rudy would go to the hospital every morning before his shift began. I went at noon, and we went together in the evenings. But the only way we could help our baby's situation was to find someone with the blood serum he needed.

Rudy's pediatrician explained that scarlet fever wasn't an epidemic at that particular moment, and that he hadn't had any recent patients to whom he could refer us. It would be completely up to us to find someone who fit the profile. We were on our own.

In those days we couldn't ask the hospital to run a database search for a match. We didn't have the Internet as a research source or as a place to post an appeal for help. Television wasn't a potential source for us—hardly anyone had one. Of course we had both newspapers and radio, but those too were closed to this sort of an appeal. The chances that we could find an adult in our own circle of acquaintances who had recovered from scarlet fever in the last two to three months seemed extremely remote. We began immediately to pass the word about what we were looking for—talking to anyone and everyone we could.

Day after day we prayed for Rudy Jr. And day after day we looked through the thick glass window at our son. His tiny body was covered with a red blotchy rash, his breathing grew raspy and labored, and his eyes were glassy. Finally, exhausted, discouraged, and in need of solace, I phoned my best friend, Linda. Between sobs I explained our plight to save Rudy. "And we've asked everywhere, every church, every store in the neighborhood. No one knows of an adult who has had it recently enough. We've talked to almost a hundred people and come up empty-handed."

Linda was quiet on the phone as she listened to me spill out my story. She waited until I paused in my sad tale to catch my breath, and then she said quietly, "Jo, maybe I can help . . ." Linda told me that she knew of someone who had recently come down with scarlet fever and who might meet the conditions we needed. Our prayers had been heard!

It took only one quick phone call and my husband dashed off in his patrol car to pick up a woman named Mrs. Etta Litner, the wife of another police officer. He sped directly to the hospital with her, and Mrs. Litner was thrilled to be able to donate her blood to make the life-saving serum for Rudy. After the serum was injected, we watched with tears streaming down our faces as we saw our son slowly regain his health. Two weeks later, we brought our boy back home.

Our family never forgot the miracle of finding a donor just

by word of mouth and through the kindness of strangers. For the next several Valentine's Days following Rudy's recovery I sent Mrs. Litner a card to express my gratitude for her gesture. And when Rudy was old enough to write, he insisted on sending the cards himself. He sent her a card on Valentine's Day every year until her death.

I believe Rudy grew up wanting to somehow repay this gift of life so freely given to him by a total stranger. Years later, Rudy decided to become a doctor, and he has given gentle care and compassionate service to many over the years. Rudy is now sixty-three, but he still hasn't lost the love and respect for elderly women that Etta Litner ignited in him so long ago. You see, I am eighty-six now, and my son Rudy visits me almost every day.

—Jo Kopfer
Belvedere, California

A Season of Growth

THE BRISK SEPTEMBER air had at last calmed my son's crying, and for a brief moment, he dozed off. The weight of his body made my thin arms ache as I carried him along the village roads. My tired, teary eyes squinted as the sun lit up the morning sky. The bright yellow school buses rumbled along past us, filled with old friends.

I didn't regret missing senior year of high school—I had surpassed all of my peers a long time ago, and their careless days and trivial activities seemed now immature and pointless to me. I was naive and full of the wonder of being a young mother. I knew that love would always see me through. Yet, it seemed so long ago that I had still had choices in my life, and for a moment as I watched the school bus filled with happy, noisy teenagers, my stomach tightened with jealousy.

When John's wet newborn body was placed into my innocent arms, my seventeen years of life had been accelerated as if by the shake of a magic wand. I entered the world of womanhood. When I looked into the mirror, my bright, youthful glow had turned into the reflection of a tired, drawn mother. The illusions of happiness a baby would bring were rapidly fading into the harsh realities of life.

I quietly sneaked up the stairs of my grandparents' house, trying not to wake them. My early morning ritual of walking the hills with John had become annoying to them, but I didn't know what else to do to make the crying stop. I was thankful for a place to live, even though it was different from my picture-perfect dreams. All during my pregnancy I had held an image of us living in a cute little cottage with flower gardens and a front porch swing, but I had to take what was offered to me and was constantly reminded not to complain.

I gently placed John on the bed, and his painful cries of hunger began immediately. I knew I had fed him his last bottle during the night and that, once again, I didn't have enough money to buy much more formula. Once, at the local supermarket, I could feel the stares as he wailed in my arms. As I counted the pennies for the formula, the cashier shook her head in disgust, and I could see the looks of pity on the faces of the other shoppers. I was a child raising a child, and I was doomed to fail.

My baby's constant crying was becoming exhausting. I rocked him for hours to the soothing sounds of my humming, and he would reach up and hold on to my long, blonde hair for comfort until we both fell asleep in the chair. I would feed him bottle after bottle, but he would just vomit it up each time. My clothes and his were permanently stained, and my depression became so great that I didn't even bother to change my clothes from day to day. My menial, part-time job never provided enough money, and there was rarely enough food. I frequently stopped by my parents' house conveniently at suppertime, hoping they would invite me to stay. I yearned for the taste of roast turkey, but I would grab just a slice of bread and tell them I was eating a big dinner later. I was afraid that if anyone really knew I was starving, they would take John away from me forever. I wasn't an unfit mother, I just wasn't prepared to deal with this overwhelming responsibility.

Weighing just eighty-five pounds, my body began to fade away, my mind felt numb, and my heart was empty. My world was spinning in circles around me, and my spirit was depleted. I was a hollow woman.

John's crying spells continued, and I couldn't stand to hear his high-pitched squeal anymore. Exhausted mentally and physically, I put him down into his crib, and even though he cried out for comfort, I didn't care. I walked away, afraid for his own security. I didn't trust myself with him anymore. I began to scream at him, telling him to give me a break, to just be quiet even for a minute. His face was soaked with tears and his T-shirt was drenched with sweat, but none of it mattered to me. I knew I was going completely crazy.

Finally, putting my crying baby into his car seat, I drove straight to my father's house. Pushing open the front door, I literally threw John into my father's arms. Looking at my desperate, weary eyes, my father knew exactly what was going through my mind. I was leaving and I was never coming back. As I ran down the driveway, I could hear John crying out for me, but I just drove away, abandoning him.

For hours I drove around the surrounding towns. The antique cottages along the shoreline seemed so perfect with their finely trimmed lawns, cobblestone driveways, and brightly colored window boxes. I wondered who lived inside these immaculate homes and what life would be like if I had been born there. I wondered if they were happy or if there was such a thing as happiness anymore. Eventually, I found myself back in my own hometown, driving past the low-income projects and watching the residents who struggled through each dreary day. I shuddered to think that I had fallen into this hopeless pattern of life. With only a high school education and my pathetic situation, I was traveling down the wrong road and taking an innocent baby with me. It had been a selfish decision to have him—I was holding on when I knew I should be letting go. I could never give to him what he needed and what he deserved. I cursed myself for being naive enough to think that love was all I needed. What once was the answer to my prayers had now become a burden.

Once home, I threw myself down on my bed and fell fast asleep. A few hours later, I was awakened by the sounds of John's cooing, and rubbing my tired eyes, I looked up to see my father standing over me. He placed John into my arms, patted my head, and walked away.

The cool breeze gently blew the curtains and I could feel the ocean mist in the air. It felt as though a fever had finally broken inside of me, and for the first time since John was born, I was thinking clearly. The few hours of sleep felt like a lifetime and rejuvenated my spirits.

I looked down at my baby, and he stared blankly back at me. For this brief peaceful moment, I thought about why there hadn't been a connection between us—I contemplated for a moment the word *bonding* and wondered where I had failed. I bent down to caress his baby-soft cheek with mine, and as I closed my eyes, my tears fell gently down on him. I could feel his tiny heart marching to his rapid breathing, and I touched his soft lips and cute dimples with my fingertips. I sat back to admire his beauty. He was perfect.

For the first time, I began to talk to him out loud. I begged for his forgiveness and promised that someday I would get my life together. I told him we were in this together and promised never to give him up. As his blue eyes began to dance and his feet began to kick, he smiled at me for the first time. He recognized me as his mother—a connection had been made. This was the sign I had been waiting for—I picked him up and squeezed him tight. My eyes filled with tears as I slowly said, "I'm your mother!"

WEARING KHAKI SHORTS and a white, short-sleeved polo shirt, John struggled to look fourteen. He was much smaller than most of his friends, but still, as he tossed his suitcase into the bus's luggage compartment, I admired the transformation and wondered where the time had gone. An honor student and president of his class, John had been chosen to lay a wreath in Arlington Cemetery with the U.S. Marines. It was his first trip to Washington, D.C. My stomach was in knots, for this would also be his first time away from me for more than one night.

His teacher gave the last call to assemble on the bus, and as he walked back toward me, I caught his eyes watering as he nervously grinned. But then there were those familiar dimples brightening his slender face as he hugged me good-bye. Stepping onto the bus, he hesitated for a minute, then turned around and ran back to me. My hands clasped his and then he gently hugged me good-bye once more. He walked away quickly, and I wiped away the tears. My son was becoming a man, and I was so proud. His face pushed against the windowpane, and I kept waving until the bus had disappeared in the distance. An admiring mother walked toward me and said, "Wow, you must be doing something right! Your son was the only student who kissed his mother good-bye."

I walked back to my car and before I drove away, I took a moment to pull out the baby picture of John that I kept hidden above the visor. I reflected upon the choices I had made. I thought about what I had given up and in the end, what I had gotten in return. Though the road had been difficult at times, we had learned to grow up together. Many of John's first experiences were also firsts for me. We depended on each other and often confided our hopes and dreams to each other. He was my strength, my best friend, and my reason for being. It was a naive teenager who had made a selfish decision fourteen years ago, yet in the end it was also a decision of great love.

— AMBER M. REILLY
Cohasset, Massachusetts

A Textbook Example

A GUST OF ICE-COLD wind pierced my face as I left the warmth of my classroom and headed across the college campus to the library, my *Medical-Surgical Nursing* textbook in hand. "Are you sure you don't want to go eat lunch with us and study for tomorrow's psychology quiz?" asked one of my fellow classmates. "That neuro exam isn't until *next* week. We can cram for that later."

I didn't understand it, but I couldn't shake the feeling that I should study the neurology nursing material today. I located a secluded spot in the library, peeled off my heavy wool coat, scarf, and gloves, and opened the text to a section of the "Neurological Nursing" chapter we hadn't yet even covered in class: the signs and symptoms of head injury. I found myself totally absorbed in the material, even imagining that I was taking care of such a patient.

I glanced at my watch and was startled to discover it was

6:30 P.M. I hadn't even stopped to eat. I was supposed to pick up my mother and sisters by 7:00 P.M. and drive to church for the midweek prayer service. Pulling into the driveway at home, I honked the horn and sat back to wait. But my family, usually so prompt, did not appear.

When I dashed up to the house to see what was delaying them, I found my mother lying across the porch steps. "I slipped on a little patch of ice, but I'm not hurt," she explained. "I think I just scraped my arm a little."

"Maybe you should go to the emergency room, just to be sure you're okay," I suggested as we helped her back into the house and onto the sofa. One sister brought an ice pack for Mother's arm and another got her a glass of ginger ale.

A short while later, Mother complained of feeling nauseated. "It's probably just the ginger ale; I'm okay, really," she insisted. "Just let me go to sleep." But then we noticed even stranger behavior. One moment she was giggling excitedly, the next she was drowsy, and the next moment, she tried to push us away, which was so unlike Mother. And there was something different about her touch, there was a certain weakness about it.

A detailed list formed in my mind as vividly as the words had appeared earlier in the afternoon on the pages of my nursing textbook. The symptoms of a head injury: nausea . . . alternating levels of consciousness . . . weakness.

I grabbed a flashlight and checked Mother's pupils. They were unequal in size and barely receptive to light. My mother was a textbook example of a patient with a head injury.

We rushed Mother to the hospital, where surgery was performed to remove a blood clot in her brain. After the operation, the neurosurgeon informed our family: "Your mother is in the intensive care unit and her condition is stable. If she had been permitted to go to bed tonight, it's very likely she would have died in her sleep."

I studied the doctor's knitted brow and grave eyes in astonishment. God had spared my mother's life.

One cold winter afternoon, my classmates had tried to convince me that we had nearly a week to prepare for our neurology nursing examination, but I had been compelled to study the material that very day, as if I were actually caring for such a patient. As it turned out, I had done just that.

—ROBERTA MESSNER
Kenova, West Virginia

Promises to Keep

I T HAS BEEN said that dreams contain riches beyond our imagination. Dreams can bring personal warnings, solutions to problems, or messages designed to nurture our spiritual growth. They can give us direction, encouragement, or information about ourselves. Yet it seems that most of the time we pay no attention and cast our dreams aside, as if they were without meaning. For my mother, however, that was not the case.

Let me begin by saying that in the early part of this century, it wasn't at all unusual for a family to have ten or twelve children, and sometimes more. Children worked together with their parents in the fields of the family farm and helped prepare food and clothing. Each person was a valued member of the family's workforce and an integral part of their survival. My mother, Mary Thomas, was the twelfth of thirteen children, and when she married Leland Jeppson, who came from a family of nine, it was pretty much assumed that they, too, would have a dozen or so children of their own. But Mary was a little ahead of the times, perhaps, and she had other plans.

Although Mary loved all of her siblings, nieces, and nephews, she also realized that there was a price to be paid by the children of a large family. While she was growing up, her family could not afford to give Mary the finer things of life, and she had a limited education. As she considered the prospect of having her own children, she came to the conclusion that if she and Leland limited their family to two children instead of twelve (as he desired), there would be more resources for those two children for the nice things of life, especially the college education that Mary had been denied and felt was so important. Her husband finally accepted her reasoning, and they were both thrilled when Mary found out she was expecting their first baby.

There was another man in Mary's life, and that was her father, Charles Rowlands Thomas. He was a very gentle and extremely intelligent man, and he had been Mary's knight in shining armor and best friend as she grew up. In his later years, he had served in the political arena and as a judge in Idaho where they lived. But about the time Mary became pregnant, her father became quite ill, and Mary's only hope was that he would live long enough to see her first child born.

One day as Mary sat at her sewing machine creating a layette for the expected baby, she noticed that it had become very dark outside, as if a big storm were approaching. It was midday, and she was waiting for Leland to come in from the fields for lunch. Feeling unusually tired, she rested her head momentarily on her arm. When she awoke a few minutes later, she realized she must have fallen asleep and was quite shaken by a dream she had had—a dream that would dramatically change her life's plan.

In her dream Mary saw a beautiful park filled with many people laughing and playing. It was cool and green, and she saw herself walking through the grass, holding the hand of a little boy on one side and a little girl on the other. The three of them were looking for a place to have a picnic. As they walked along, happily talking, she noticed a group of children in the distance who were watching her. As they grew closer, she saw that they looked rather unkempt and hungry, and quite neglected. Anxious to enjoy the day and get on with her picnic, she tried to ignore these children but kept feeling their longing eyes fixed on her and her two well-dressed and well-cared-for children. Mary finally felt compelled to walk over and speak to them, asking why they were there and where their parents were.

One of the children in the group said simply, "We were supposed to be your children, but you didn't want us."

The child's words, which played over and over again in her head after she awoke, so disturbed Mary that she immediately went to Leland for comfort. She and Leland together made the decision to accept any and all children the Good Lord would send them. In recalling the dream, Mary never could tell exactly how many children were in the group, but she did remember that there seemed to be an equal number of boys and girls.

Not long afterward, Mary's beloved father passed away, just days short of being able to see her first child. Mary felt as though she had lost her hero, her closest friend, and the man who had been her spiritual guide throughout her life.

The years passed, and before long there were five young children in the Jeppson household. Times were tough, and when a flood eventually destroyed the fruit orchards on their little farm, the family decided to move to Cardston, Canada, to take advantage of a new business venture. Although desperately homesick for her native country and the folks back home, Mary continued to raise her growing family despite difficult living conditions. She worked hard and never complained about her lot in life as she accepted, with open arms and great love, each new baby that came into their family.

The Depression was in full swing as over the next few years Mary gave birth to six more children, including a pair of twin girls who died at about a week old, unable to survive the freezing conditions in Canada. Mary and Leland, never going back on their promise to welcome as many little souls as possible into their lives, now had eleven, nine living. Each was taught to work hard and contribute to the family's welfare. Although Mary still believed very strongly in her children's receiving an education, their farm was miles from the nearest school and their only form of transportation was by horseback. Every morning she would put two children on each horse, and the two (and eventually three) horses would take them to school and back through the icy wind and snow. The children, wrapped in blankets, put hot rocks in their boots to keep their feet from freezing during their journey, placed the rocks in a warm stove at school during the day, and put them back into their boots for the ride home. As Mary watched her children ride off each morning, she thought about how different the scene was from the one in her mind's eye many years before when she dreamed of the fine education her two children would receive.

Eventually, Mary and Leland moved back to Idaho, and shortly thereafter, one more baby was born. This was their twelfth child, including the twins who had passed away—exactly the dozen children Leland had originally desired. The older girls were now graduating from high school and the boys were entering the army to fight in World War II; times continued to be difficult, and Mary and Leland finally felt certain they would not be having any more children. But then Mary, who was now past forty, suffered a miscarriage, and her weakened, worn-out body simply collapsed. Lying unconscious in a hospital, without modern medical procedures or blood transfusions, she was unable to rally for many weeks.

It was during this time in the hospital that my mother, Mary Jeppson, had another very unusual experience—one that would be difficult to explain to others but that she knew in her heart had actually occurred. She later told her family that as she lay unconscious she was visited by her father, who had died almost twenty years earlier. He sat next to her bed in a chair and held a large book on his lap. She was somehow aware that he was looking through the book—a scrapbook of sorts—and he would nod and smile gently as he slowly turned the pages and studied each one carefully.

After some time, Mary's father finally came to the end of the book and was looking at the last page when he turned to her and said with great compassion, "Mary, it's your decision: you can come with me if you want and we'll close this book for good. Your body is weak and worn out, and if you are too tired to continue on, you can leave with me now. However, I must tell you that there is still one more child that was promised to your family."

Mary remembered feeling an overwhelming desire to be with him, to be relieved of her body's pain and her life's hardships. But as he stood up to leave, Mary noticed two doors in the distance beyond him, and she could see a radiant light coming from underneath the doors. He looked back one more time and again told her she could come with him or stay and bring forth the child who was waiting to join her family. She lay motionless as she watched him tenderly wave good-bye, and then he was gone.

When Mary eventually regained consciousness, she came back to a very frail and painful body, and it took many months for her strength to be restored. The beautiful experience with her father remained locked in her heart for a long time, but when she finally confided it to her husband, he responded that he, too, felt there was one more child waiting.

And almost six years later, Mary was pregnant once again. On her first visit to the doctor, he suggested that she was too old and her body too weak to carry a baby and that perhaps she should consider terminating the pregnancy. Mary looked him in the eyes and answered sternly, "If you knew what I have given up to bring this child into the world, you wouldn't even suggest that." This last child was born almost twenty-five years to the day after the birth of Mary's first child. She named the baby Marian. I was Mary and Leland's thirteenth child and their seventh girl.

Mary's son Ralph would later write of his mother:

To me, Mary Jeppson is not just a "Mother of the Year" but one of those creatures who come along only rarely. In her own way, she has fit perfectly into our civilization. She has accepted what she could not change, she changed what she could, and in the process, made the earth a better place in which to live for all those who have come in contact with her.

My mother saw all of her children grow up to become successful and happy people, even without the expensive education or elegant clothes she originally hoped for. But by the end of her life, she knew one thing: her large and beloved "picnic dream" family had, indeed, brought riches beyond her imagination.

— MARIAN JEPPSON WALKER
South Jordan, Utah

An Angel of My Own

W HEN I WAS a small boy my family lived on the North Side of Chicago. My mama, my papa, and my four siblings all lived together in a small apartment in the bustling heart of the city. It was kind of a tough neighborhood, but we kids enjoyed it—we ruled the streets with our games of kick the can and stickball.

Our lives followed a set pattern every day. First, Papa would leave for work at the break of dawn, trying to tiptoe out of the little flat so as not to wake the rest of us. Once awake, the older kids, Mary, Tony, and Joe, would busy themselves getting ready to take the trolley to school. I was too young for school then, so I had to stay home with Mama and the little baby. I didn't really stay home, of course. Most of the time I was outside the apartment building playing with the other kids my age, all too young to go to school but too old to want to stay inside with babies. And each afternoon I would leave my pals and run down to the corner where the trolley stopped. I'd be there waiting when Mary, Tony, and Joe all piled off. I couldn't wait for the day when it would finally be my turn, too, to get on that old trolley and ride to school like a big kid.

But there was one warm and sunny Chicago day when my mother would not let me go outside to play. "Why not, Mama?" I pleaded. "I don't want to stay inside all day!"

"I'm not sure," she admitted. "Just a feeling I have. I want you to stay inside with me today." And all day long she kept me busy with small tasks, everything from shelling fava beans and peeling potatoes to rolling out biscotti dough—anything to keep me inside as long as the ominous feeling persisted within her.

At last the long indoor afternoon was ending. I could see from the clock that it was time for me to go down and meet the trolley. I put on my little cloth cap and jacket and reached for the door. "Rocco, no!" My mother shouted, running toward me. "I don't want you to meet your brothers and sister today. Instead, I want you to . . . take a nap."

A nap? I was six years old! Why should I take a nap at my age? But she insisted, pulling off my hat and coat and ushering me into my bedroom. She watched from the doorway as I reluctantly climbed into bed and closed my eyes. Then she quietly shut the door and tiptoed away.

And then something incredible happened. As soon as I rested my head on my pillow a burst of white light filled the room, temporarily blinding me. When the spectacular light began to fade, I could see the most glorious angel at the foot of my bed. Every detail was clear—the angel appeared to have shining wings and was crowned with a golden halo. He hovered lightly in the air a few feet away from me, with his arms outstretched in a loving way. I felt a warmth spreading throughout my body, a feeling of pure love and complete security. It was not frightening, it was glorious. The vision lasted only a minute or two, but the intensity of that feeling has stayed with me my whole life. When the angel left my room I rested my head on my pillow once again, enveloped in a feeling of serenity and joy.

Not long after this incredible experience, I heard the sounds of my brothers and sister running up the wooden stairs. They burst into the apartment with great cries of excitement. "Mama, Mama!" they called out. "It was so exciting! You should have seen what happened. A trolley car slipped off of its tracks and skidded into the corner telephone pole at Race Street. You know the corner, Mama, the corner where Rocco waits for us each day. It's lucky he wasn't there today, Mama!"

Mama said nothing, but her eyes welled with tears and she bent her head in silent prayer. I opened the door of my bedroom and whispered, "Mama, Mama, come here!" Wiping her eyes on the corner of her apron, she entered my room. "Right there, Mama. He was right there!" I pointed to the foot of my bed. "It was an angel that came. An angel of my own that came to protect me!" Abandoning herself to her emotions, Mama sank to her knees and put her arms around me. "Oh, Rocco, I didn't know what might happen today," she sobbed. "All I knew was that I needed to keep you near me, to keep you safe." And safe she kept me, safe at home with my own magnificent guardian angel.

— ROCCO FRANCISCO
San Jose, California

The Gift of Hope

W E DIDN'T GET to hear our oldest son's first cry, but the obstetrician later told us that it was actually a strangled scream. On February 11, 1989, our son was delivered by emergency C-section due to fetal distress. I was under general anesthesia, and my husband was waiting anxiously outside the operating room.

My baby's lungs were full of meconium—that first sticky, dark green bowel movement that is usually released by infants shortly after birth. But fetal distress caused our son to release it while still in my uterus, and it polluted the previously sterile amniotic fluid. The meconium became embedded in our tiny son's lungs.

I came out of an anesthetic stupor and looked around. The OR was quiet and empty, except for a lone nurse fiddling with a surgical tray. There was a dull ache in my abdomen, and I felt dizzy. My husband was standing at the door to the OR. He moved close to me when he saw I was awake.

"What did we have?" I asked weakly.

"A little boy," my husband said. He seemed subdued.

"I'm so sorry it didn't work out like we planned," I ventured, referring to the C-section.

"It doesn't matter," my husband assured me. "What matters now is that our son needs to recover. He is very sick. He was rushed into the neonatal intensive care unit."

"Oh, God!" I cried. As my husband continued to explain the circumstances to me, I pleaded, over and over, "Oh, God, please save my baby."

Because I developed a fever after the surgery, it was more than a day later when I finally got to see my baby. He lay still and sedated on an open warming table, his fragile newborn body invaded by tubes and needles. He was beautiful. A dark black fuzz of hair framed his round face, and long dark lashes brushed his pale cheeks.

My husband stood near me as tears rolled down my cheeks, and I sang a lullaby softly to my son. I talked to him and I prayed. I was so young, only nineteen, and with all my heart and soul, I wanted my baby to live.

But the neonatologist told us that the prognosis was very poor. There had been absolutely no change in the baby's condition since he was born. He was alive only because of the respirator and the other life-giving equipment that surrounded his tiny body. And when our pediatrician heard that I was pumping and storing milk, she told my family to talk to me about it.

"Somebody has to prepare her. That baby is probably not

going to make it." Nobody had the heart to give me her message. But I was not naive. I knew how serious my son's condition was; I just refused to give up hope. Five times a day I sat down with my breast pump, and as I pumped the milk I bargained with God. "God, I'm doing what I can for this baby. Now you do your part."

When our son was nine days old my husband and I came into the NICU for our daily visit.

"Oh, no!" I said to the nurse. "What's the matter with him?" The baby was gray, and his body looked as shriveled as an old man's. The nurse didn't answer, but she offered to wrap him up so we could hold him. We knew this meant the end was near. Until then we had not been allowed even to touch him.

She wrapped the baby up, wires and all, in a soft cotton blanket and placed him in my arms. He felt light as a feather. My husband leaned over my shoulder to get closer to his son. The nurse used a Polaroid camera to take our first family picture. As my husband and I held him we talked to him, and begged him to live.

"I want you so much, Little Lamb," I said.

That night I sang to my son and kissed him good night. We tore ourselves away from him and went home. When I arrived at the NICU the next morning, the nurses grabbed me and hugged me, and actually danced me to my son's crib. He was awake, his cheeks looked filled out, and they were pink. He looked up at me with the dark eyes I had never yet seen.

"It's a miracle," we were told. "During the night your son's vital signs picked up dramatically and he even started trying to breathe on his own. We were able to turn the respirator down from 100 percent to 60 percent."

But he wasn't happy. He struggled against the respirator, turning his little head back and forth, trying to free himself from the pipe sticking down his throat. His mouth opened in soundless wails. My heart wrenched for him, but as soon as I held his hand and started singing to him, he calmed down. He looked up at me and blinked his eyes, and soon he fell back to sleep.

Convinced that my baby responded so favorably to the voice he had come to know over the last nine months, the nurses suggested that I sing into a little cassette recorder so they could turn it on for him when I wasn't in the unit. We bought a minirecorder and I sang lullabies and soothing folk songs until I filled up an entire tape. I sang every song I knew—all the tunes I had been humming to myself throughout my pregnancy. The nurses told me that every time they turned on the recorder, the baby would calm down and cease his struggling. It was reassuring to know that I made such a difference in my son's well-being. I had felt so helpless until then. But now I felt useful and necessary. Even though my son was still ill, we were filled with joy. He was going to make it. As he turned two weeks old, he was finally removed from the respirator.

We were now able to share in his care. We diapered him, sponged him, and took turns holding him. And the milk I had expressed for him was administered through a feeding tube. I felt jubilant that I could finally care for my son.

At three weeks he graduated to getting my milk from a bottle. When I fed him the first time he gulped the milk down with gusto and then let the nipple slide from his mouth. He looked straight into my eyes and smiled.

When he was four weeks old I was able to breast-feed him. The nurses warned me that it would probably be a struggle. Many babies develop nipple confusion if they are not breast-fed soon after birth. But my baby latched right on and cuddled into my breast. He started gaining his weight back, and he was soon transferred to the nursery. A week later we brought him home, completely healthy and back to his birth weight of six pounds, twelve ounces.

Although the first month of my son's life was precarious, I never gave up hope. Hope was the one ray of sunshine in the dark shadows of my life. I knew that when hope was gone, so too was the life force. And if hope was kept alive, so too was our determination to go on.

The whole family joined us in celebrating his circumcision, his *bris*, when he was officially named. He was named after my grandfather, Nathaniel, and we all thought it was so appropriate. Nathaniel means "a gift from God." And our son is a very precious gift indeed.

— SURIE FETTMAN
Brooklyn, New York

Picture Perfect

THE BABY'S SCREAM from the bathroom stopped my heart. I raced in, horrified to think what I might find. My six-year-old, Amy, who was trying to be extra helpful to me during my uncomfortable pregnancy, had decided that she would bathe my toddler. I had asked her to turn on the bathwater, but she decided to take it a little further. She filled the tub about three inches deep just as she had seen me do many times, took Shaun's clothes off, and gently put him in the tub. When I reached him, he was standing in three inches of scalding hot water. Amy had inadvertently turned on just the hot tap, and Shaun's tiny feet were being burned.

I grabbed him, threw him into the sink, and instantly turned on the cold water to stop the burning. In a moment of panic and anger, I turned to Amy and said, "How could you do this? Look how badly you've burned his feet!" Amy ran from the bathroom in tears, and for the next ten minutes, I took care of Shaun's little feet. When I realized he was all right and the burn wasn't as bad as I had thought at first, I went looking for Amy. She was nowhere to be found until finally I heard her whimpers coming from underneath her bed. Amy's tender feelings had been injured more seriously than her brother's feet, and I felt terrible.

As I tried to coax her out from under the bed, I begged for her forgiveness. I tried to explain that I hadn't meant what I had said and that I had been reacting out of fear. No matter how hard I tried, she would not come out from hiding. Since I was seven months pregnant, even getting down on the floor took some negotiating; crawling under the bed to pull her out was out of the question. So I stretched my arm as far as it would go to try and reach her. Just as my hand brushed against her, she jerked her head, and somehow a prong on my wedding ring scratched her face. When she cried out and grabbed her cheek, I thought my heart would break.

She finally crawled out, and I saw what I had done. It was horrible—the scratch was about three inches long, and even though it wasn't deep, it was red and swollen and bleeding. I grabbed an ice pack and held her in my arms, both of us weeping now. I was furious at myself for hurting not only Amy's feelings but also her pretty face. To make the situation even worse, I remembered that the next day at school was "picture day" and Amy had been looking forward to it for days. Now her adorable smile would be overshadowed by a big, red swollen scratch.

When she awoke the next morning the scratch was still obvious. I iced it one more time and sent her on her way. I waited nervously over the next few weeks. Even though Amy had seemingly forgotten the incident, I was still bothered by it and dreaded seeing the picture. Even though I hadn't intended to scratch her, I knew the picture would serve as a constant reminder of my angry words that had precipitated the accident and left such an indelible mark on her spirit. I had hurt my most precious possession—my child—and felt very sad whenever I thought about it.

And then the day came when Amy rushed in from school holding her picture packet tightly in her hand. I knew she was excited, but I opened the envelope slowly, wanting to postpone the inevitable. What happened in the next instant was something for which I have no explanation; it was a miracle of the purest form. For there on Amy's school picture was a little girl with a beautiful smile and creamy, flawless skin. I examined it over and over—there was no mark of any kind on her face. It was simply gone.

We had told no one of the incident. We knew the photographer hadn't removed it—with the thousands of schoolchildren photographed, touch-ups were never part of the package. But there she was—my precious daughter—happy, perfect, beautiful. As if nothing had ever happened the night before. Now, twenty years later, the eight-by-ten copy of that picture still hangs in our home, a treasure to my heart.

Motherhood is the most demanding and emotionally taxing thing I've ever done. Like most mothers, I often become exhausted and frustrated and occasionally do or say things I later regret. I don't know who provided the sweet miracle that day the picture came home, but for all the years since, it has been a symbol of the fact that someone is watching out

for mothers, making the road a little smoother when we occasionally come to the end of our rope. And as I continue to
struggle through the everyday challenges of motherhood, it
serves as a gentle reminder to look heavenward for the example of a perfect parent who loves with a perfect love.

— HOPE GARDNER
Mesa, Arizona

Letters from Home

ROGER'S FIFTH-GRADE class was going to the California foothills for an overnight field trip as part of their study of the California gold rush. The five-day adventure allowed them to take only those items that were actually used or eaten around 1848. The teachers sent the parents a secret note asking us to write our child a letter as if we lived in the 1840s, and our child was indeed going off to "Californ-eye-ay" to find gold. The letters would arrive by "pony express" that night in the gold country, giving each child a personal welcome.

I jumped into the project. My own family history puts all four of my great-grandfathers in California before 1848 with a rich heritage of ranching and mining. Some relatives came across the country on horseback, others sailed around the horn of South America and landed in San Francisco. More followed. For me, this would be an easy assignment.

I journeyed back in time in my mind's eye to find words for my gold-seeking son. I wanted to gently remind him of his roots, to confirm his moral foundation in a new strange land. I started with a sentimental picture:

> The morning glory vine grows 'round your upstairs window, son, and the flowers seem to love the morning light. Banjo still chases the chickens when I go out every morning for eggs. Everyone here asks about you, and your absence is sorely felt.

The letter continued with news those of us still at home who loved him dearly:

> Your brother shot a skunk in the shed last night and learned the hard way not to do that again. He says if you'd been here he would have made a better plan. He prefers to sleep in your bed.

I also wanted to affirm my son's wings of manhood, courage, and individual vision:

> I am so proud of you for making such a hard trip and for having the courage to follow your dreams. You have always been strong and able, and a good thinker.

But I couldn't resist parental concern:

> Don't smoke or spend time with drink or gamblers. Wear your woollies and warm socks, Roger. Pray and go

to church when you can. Your Father in Heaven watches over you.

And of course,

> We all love you, son. You are missed. We pray for you nightly. All our love, Mother.

Finally, I soaked the letter in brown tea water and rubbed dirt into it to age the paper, and placed it in a handmade envelope.

Feeling satisfied and somewhat sentimental, I spent the evening in newfound appreciation for my ancestors whose courage and perseverance gave me the land I loved today. I also realized that my life needed courage, too, for the very same reasons my ancestors did, just under different circumstances. Our family trait of stubbornness suddenly took on dignity.

Suddenly, I had an inspiration. I remembered some old letters in the family files from an ancestor to her son. I could use a real 150-year-old address for my letter to Roger! I hadn't really read these old letters—the handwriting was faded and hard to decipher. But now as I began to study them, I started seeing through the eyes of my great-great-great-grandmother Antiss, from Hardwich, Massachusetts, whose son Daniel rode cross-country to the cries of gold in California. Son Barnabas traveled by ship. I was surprised by my own emotions.

The heartache I vicariously felt thinking of her sons going off to an unknown land was wrenching. But I also sensed her inner strength—the strength that is reserved for women during childbirth, war, sickness, and death that enables them to carry on. The same strength that enables them to endure the inevitable weaning—the anxious paradox of wanting to give your child roots *and* wings. It is the energy of life that mothers try to give their children: Go! Explore! Create! But don't forget to write.

The letters were dated from September 1843 to August 1850. By now, they were 140 years old. I was stunned as I read:

> I have read your letter and happy to hear you are well and still continue to be good, dutiful and obedient. I should have sent you some stockings but have not had time to knit them, so you must wear out what you have . . . read your bible everyday.
>
> Be good boys and never give me course for sorrow & when you reprove each other do it in kindness. I hope you will be careful of your health and avoid all injurious habits such as smoking, for in reality I think it worse than any other. If your health should fail which I trust will not, then it would be the care of a mother you would need.
>
> I trust you have been good and kind among your friends but fear you will never realize your ideas of gold, if you do not, it makes no difference with me, you are my own dear boy and can obtain an honest livelihood.
>
> [As a widow] it is humiliating enough to feel as though I was a burden to friends but it is my fortune and I desire to be patient under it, but one thing I am thankful for is, I have not always to stay here. Although I

enjoy the world and it looks pleasant to me, I look forward to a far better place. I trust in God, and feel though afflictions were good for me it has shown me the vanity of setting my heart on earthly objects.

And now may the blessing of heaven attend you and the prayers of your mother will be offered continually to our Heavenly Father who has thus far protected you from harm. Yours in much affection, Antiss Ross

Here was my letter, my heart—my own joys, my same sorrows. I was a 1990s "widow" (divorcee), and for two weeks a month my children were separated from me and our bonds disconnected. I too lived with a longing for earthly objects and security. I too felt I was a burden to friends as I got on my feet. And I too have counseled my children to stay close to their Heavenly Father. My great-great-great-grandmother had gone before me in joy, affliction, trust, and faith. Separated by more than a century, we were simply two mothers who sang the same song.

Her tender admonishments, painful longings, and selfless hopes in her boys would eventually uproot Antiss. In the spring of 1851, she sold all her belongings and sailed for San Francisco to eventually join her sons. She died a few months later on November 5, undoubtedly having found "the better place"—where she would surely be reunited with her boys someday. Neither son struck it rich in the gold fields, though Daniel stayed in San Francisco and founded Fulton Iron Works, which built the first ferry on San Francisco Bay and serviced the shipping, mining, railroad, and architectural trades. Barnabas went south to Santa Barbara. They each married and had families, and eventually one of those families became mine.

Reading the letters that night gave me a new understanding of the past. It also gave me hope for the future and the courage, as a mother, to make my own history.

— MARY GRAYSON
San Francisco, California

Delayed Gratification

ANY WOMAN WHO has dealt with infertility knows the painful longing that accompanies that condition. When my husband and I decided it was time to think about having a baby, I never dreamed it would be a ten-year venture with infertility doctors, consultants, and lawyers. Although I was brought up in a very loving family, I was an only child, and I always wanted several children of my own when I married.

Unfortunately, my mother had taken the fertility hormone DES (diethylstilbestrol) when she was pregnant with me, which was later linked to numerous medical problems in women, ranging from ovarian cancer to infertility. But because my mother was no longer alive, much of the medical information vital to my condition was unavailable. After my husband, Ben, and I had tried for nine months to conceive, I knew deep down that having a baby of our own would be a long ordeal.

> *. . . the sweet smell of baby's skin, Mother Goose and*
> Sesame Street, *pink ruffled dresses and miniature overalls,*
> *toy trains and dollhouses, little hands pressed in plaster . . .*

The first year consisted of fertility drugs coupled with artificial insemination. We felt certain this would work and were discouraged when it failed. In vitro fertilization (IVF) was then suggested, which is a process where the woman is injected with fertility drugs to enable her body to produce an increased number of eggs (typically a woman produces one per cycle; with the drug, she can produce ten to twenty). The eggs are retrieved and fertilized outside the body, then placed back in her womb. Our first try with this method was successful, and we were ecstatic. I was very careful, feeling so lucky finally to be pregnant, but I unfortunately miscarried twins at eleven weeks.

The disappointment was unimaginable, but that same year, I went through two more IVFs; one was an unsuccessful fertilization and the other time I miscarried. After so many months of hoping and praying, living by my cycle, doctor visits, blood tests, and discouraging phone calls, I knew that my mind and body needed a break from the treatments.

> *. . . lollipops and licorice, infectious giggles on a carousel*
> *ride, peekaboo and patty cake, popped balloons and spilled*
> *milk, bubble baths . . .*

For the next two years, both my husband and I changed jobs and settled into a life of two working professionals. If we couldn't be parents quite yet, we would be successful in our careers. After a move to Baltimore, we decided to look into treatments again, as well as the possibility of adoption. So, back to the same grind of injections, tests, doctor's appointments—but all with the same disheartening results: no baby.

In the meantime, we had some very dear friends, Kathy and Shawn, who had just had their second baby, a boy. They already had a three-year-old daughter, and Ben and I were their children's godparents. When we visited their home near Seattle to attend the new baby's christening, Kathy made it clear that she and Shawn felt satisfied with their family and didn't intend to have any more children. They offered to carry a baby for us if we got to the point where we might consider using a gestational carrier. Deeply grateful for their offer of love, we told them that we hadn't given up completely on trying ourselves, but that we would think about it.

We investigated adoption but learned that the average cost in the state of Maryland was between $18,000 and $25,000. We were shocked and again discouraged, as that was out of the financial picture for us. After six more laborious and unsuccessful IVF attempts, with spirits depleted, I finally picked up the phone and made the most difficult call of my life. It was a cold, clear January morning when I poured my heart out to my dear friend Kathy, and asked if she would still be willing to carry a baby for me. What a feeling to know there was someone in the world with enough love and sympathy in her heart to offer such a gift! I would be eternally and profoundly grateful.

. . . bicycles with training wheels, chocolate fingerprints on every wall, butterfly kisses and caterpillars in jars, night-lights and lullabies, stomping through autumn leaves . . .

With renewed hope, we began the process of having frozen embryos of mine sent overnight to a Seattle fertility clinic. Kathy would have to make a two-hour drive every day for two weeks for the procedure, which she did—graciously, generously sacrificing time with her family so that her friend might *have* a family. It was May 1997, and at the same time Kathy was trying to get pregnant with my embryos, I was also giving it "one last try" at home. I figured with both of us working at it, certainly something magic would happen.

No luck. Kathy and I were both unsuccessful, and for the four months following that sad time, Ben and I were dazed, numb, almost mournful. We had used all our options—we had now been trying for nine years and we were at the end of the road.

. . . dimpled cheeks and dimpled legs, toes so tiny and soft you want to eat them . . .

Our insurance was also running out. I had been covered for the very expensive IVF treatments, but the coverage would end in December that year. Because Kathy was so willing and so encouraging, we opted to let her try one more time before the end of the year. So in October, our good doctor in Baltimore was more than willing, once again, to perform the necessary procedure to retrieve, fertilize, freeze, and ship my eggs to Seattle. Ben and I agreed that this would be our last (the eleventh!) try at IVF. If it didn't work this time, we would somehow accept the grave reality that God didn't intend for us to have a family of our own; we would be grateful for what we had and devote our life to each other and to our extended family.

> . . . *sand castles and circus clowns, growth charts and baby books, hopscotch and finger paints, a gummy "I Love You, Mommy" on the first homemade Valentine, delicious hugs and kisses every hour, every day, for the rest of your life . . .*

But at the last minute there was a hitch with the insurance company. It seems there was a regulation stating that in the case where a gestational carrier is being used, two embryos (of the normal ten to twelve retrieved) must be implanted in the real mother (a "good faith" act, of sorts) while the other embryos are given to the carrier. Although we had hoped all the frozen embryos could be sent to Seattle for Kathy's use, we, of course, complied with the policy.

While we awaited news of Kathy's IVF results, I was scheduled, as is routine in the IVF process, for a pregnancy test. The appointment fell on the day after Thanksgiving. Normally in an IVF, four to six embryos were implanted in me; this time, because it was just an insurance requirement, there were only two, and I knew my chances of becoming pregnant were slim to none. So as I set out at 5:30 A.M. that morning on the two-hour drive for my blood test for pregnancy, I wondered why I was even bothering.

After arriving home many hours later, I answered the

phone to a nurse's voice telling me—incredibly—that I was pregnant, that my blood hormone levels were fantastic, and that I should consider this a probable "keeper"—a true gift! Weeks later, when Ben and I heard the rapid little beat of our baby's heart through the doctor's stethoscope, we could hardly control our tears. We knew this baby was a gift from God—the result of ten years of persistence, prayers, and great love.

My dear friend Kathy could curtail her noble efforts. Ben and I would have our baby's sweet smell and giggles on the carousel after all. The price we had paid through our prolonged trial and our tears would be small payment, indeed, for the beautiful, warm bundle of a very healthy Benjamin George Cameransi III, born August 2, 1998.

— PATRICIA K. CAMERANSI
Hershey, Pennsylvania

I Gave God a Picture

CHICAGO WAS UNSEASONABLY warm for February; a sweatshirt was enough to keep out the chill. Another session of swimming lessons had ended, and I had invited three young swimmers and their mothers over for pizza.

While Georgia, Lynn, and I talked, our four kids chased one another around the house. My seven-year-old son, Alex, who always enjoyed costumes, was dressed like a king in a maroon bathrobe belted around a wooden sword.

But it was a school night, and soon the fun was over. "Time to go home!" we moms yelled. After Georgia and her children left, Lynn and I focused on finding and separating our own boys. But they were nowhere to be found.

That wasn't unusual. Like all seven-year-old boys, Alex and Zack had a hard time bringing playtime to an end. They would rather hide in a closet or under a bed than obey a summons home. But tonight, we looked everywhere in my century-old two-flat: in every closet, every nook and cranny, under the front porch and the back, upstairs and down. We looked in the garage and in the alley. And then we decided to call the police.

The boys were gone. And we hadn't a clue about where or why.

I live in Chicago, about six miles north of the Loop. Although I am a native Californian, I've felt at home here for years. I've adopted urban habits and grown comfortable raising Alex among alleys, big streets, and high-rises.

But with my son lost somewhere in the city, my sense of security vanished.

The police came quickly and peppered us with questions. Who were the boys' friends? Where did they hang out? Were they upset about something? Were there any family problems? Had they run away? Their questions became more personal when they discovered that Alex's father and I were divorced. Could his father have taken him? What was their relationship like? Their relationship was fine, I assured them, and no, his father hadn't kidnapped him! Furthermore, there was no way these kids had wandered off just to go to McDonald's or to visit a friend. These were highly supervised children who didn't know where to go and wouldn't know how to get there anyway. They wouldn't just sneak off. It wasn't like them, I insisted.

Which left one possibility—they had run outside for just a moment and been abducted.

That idea really made me panic. Who would've taken them? Would I ever see Alex again? Would I ever sit with him at night, stroke his hair, listen to his questions, or tell him stories of my own? Our favorite bedtime topic was disasters: the *Titanic* and the *Hindenburg,* doomed ships like the *Eastman* and the *Edmund Fitzgerald.* Reflecting on disaster is a tradition in my family. Alex often calls me "Daughter of Mrs. Disaster"—Mrs. Disaster being my own mother, whose awful stories of the misfortunes of others reinforce our family's sense of luck and fortune.

But the middle of my own disaster was no time to dwell on statistics or scenarios, awful pictures of heartbreak, and doom. I decided to pray. And so God would know who the prayers were for, I gave him a picture—a vision of a little boy tucked in his bed, home from an adventure and safe from all harm.

All night I concentrated on that picture. I never once let it leave my mind. I figured if visualization could help athletes deliver flawless performances and the wealth-minded reach their income goals, it could bring Alex home. It had worked once before when, eager to secure tickets to a sold-out opera, I imagined myself seated and smiling as the conductor raised his baton and the curtain rose. But a seat at the opera is nothing compared to the life of a child.

I prayed. I pictured. And I telephoned. I called every parent in the neighborhood and asked them to check their porches and backyards. I circled the area in a squad car, checking McDonald's, the local school, the twenty-four-hour supermarket. I listened to the police broadcast Alex's and Zack's descriptions in an all-points bulletin. With every phone call to a neighbor asking for assistance, with every block I covered in the back of a squad car, I saw a picture of my little boy in his own bed.

Three hours later, a call came in from the Town Hall Police Station. The boys had turned up in a convenience store near Wrigley Field, about twenty blocks south. It didn't take long for the police to match two tired, coatless seven-year-olds to the description on the police radio, although it seemed like forever before they pulled up to my building in a squad car.

In front of their parents, the police questioned the boys to discover where they'd been, why they'd gone, and whether they had encountered anyone on the way. Had they accepted a ride? Been in anyone's apartment? No. They had walked.

They walked because they had been playing and didn't want to stop. First, they hid under the porch. Then they hid in the alley. And then, because they knew they were in trouble, they started walking around the neighborhood, visiting the backyards of friends. When it seemed that no matter what they did, they would get in trouble, Alex suggested that they walk to his father's house in the suburb of Evanston. Except they went in the wrong direction. And even if they had been going the right way, they wouldn't have gotten there until morning.

Over the course of three hours, they meandered past homeless shelters and drop-in centers, corners where drugs are sold, bodies are traded, and conflicts are settled with knives. (Just an hour after they passed one intersection, someone was shot and killed in a drug deal gone sour.) In the end, when they were tired and hungry, longing for their beds, and not at all sure what to do next, a store owner gave them each an apple and called the police. And they were returned unscathed.

Alex is eleven now, but we both still remember the terror of that night. He remembers what it feels like to be frightened and alone, unsure how to get himself and his friend home. I remember vacillating between my fear that I'd never see my little boy again and my conviction that with God's help, I would. I remember the miracle of community: the concern and care of friends, neighbors, police officers, and strangers doing their best to get two children safely home. I remember the miracle of faith: the certainty that God watched over Alex and Zack on their nighttime journey, guiding them away from trouble and toward people who would help. And most of all, I remember that when it was over, I got to see the picture in my prayer: a tired little boy, peacefully asleep in his own bed.

— ANNE BASYE
Chicago, Illinois

Mother's Helpers

MANY CHILDREN HAVE imaginary friends; child psychologists say it's a very normal part of their development. When my daughter Tiffani was three years old, she started talking to two imaginary friends that she called Chauncey and Tetet. They played all kinds of games and went everywhere together. I didn't think much of this—I thought it was kind of cute to hear her talk to her two playmates. But on July 10, 1996, a very unusual event occurred that proved to me what special friends these two actually were.

We woke up that morning to our regular routine of getting dressed and cleaning up the house. We played a few games together, and then I put Davis, my six-month-old son, down for a nap. At lunchtime, Tiffani helped me make sandwiches and chips, and then asked if we could have a picnic out on the balcony. It was such a beautiful day that I said it would be a wonderful idea. Out the door we went, carrying plates, cups, napkins, and Tiffani's doll tucked under my arm. We all sat down around the table—Tiffani, me, the doll, and, of course, Chauncey and Tetet. We were having a lovely time chatting about the noisy blue jay that haunts our home with his loud chirping when I thought I heard Davis crying. I told Tiffani to be good while I checked on the baby, and that I would be right back. Her reply was "Don't worry, Mommy, my friends are here." I smiled at her, picked up our plates, and went in the house.

I put the plates on the sink and looked at the couch, where Davis was still peacefully sleeping. It seemed that only a minute had passed when I heard a very unusual thud coming from the balcony area. I guess in my heart I knew what had happened, but I prayed I was wrong. I ran to the door and looked out. Tiffani was not on the balcony. My heart was pounding as I took the few steps across the patio and looked over the twenty-foot drop to see my little girl lying motionless on the dirt below.

I flew down the stairs to the basement, saying over and over, "Please, let my baby be alive, please!" As soon as I opened the back door, I heard a faint whimper, which sounded like heavenly music to my ears. I had just completed an emergency training course two weeks earlier (an inspiration, I believe), and so, instead of picking her up right away, I did a quick head-to-toe assessment, as the instructor had taught us to do. Upon finding all her bones intact and no complaint of any head, back, or neck pain, I gently picked her up in my arms and just sat there crying. After a couple of minutes, we made our way into the house and up the stairs to the rocking chair.

Not wanting to let her go to sleep for fear of concussion, I cuddled and talked to her for a long time. After about twenty minutes, she started complaining that her stomach was hurting. My first thought was that it might be internal bleeding. I called the hospital and they instructed me to bring her right in. I alerted my husband and parents, packed up Tiffani and Davis, and headed out on the longest fifteen-minute drive of my life. After the doctor examined and X-rayed her, he informed us that there was no discernible internal bleeding and that we should take her home and keep an eye on her.

Later that afternoon I allowed Tiffani to take a nap. She slept peacefully for a while but then woke up crying, complaining again about her stomach. She could stand up but couldn't bend forward. I called the hospital again, and they instructed me to take her to Primary Children's Hospital for a CAT scan and other tests. Once there, Tiffani remained quite calm until the moment they strapped her down to do the CAT scan. Then she started crying, begging me to help her. I stood there, trying to be strong but feeling so helpless; I thought my heart would break. I kept asking myself over and over, Why did I leave her? Why did she fall off the balcony? She had never done anything like that before; why now?

After I held Tiffani down for more blood tests, all the while reassuring her that things would be okay as she cried in my arms, she finally fell into a deep sleep. I looked over at my parents, who had been there to support me the whole time. Emotionally exhausted, I reached out to them and cried in their arms. My mother looked at me and said, "I know Tiffani is going to be all right. I don't know how to explain it, but I just feel she is going to be fine." Her words touched my heart and I knew they were true. I was finally able to feel peace.

Tiffani was released at 2 A.M. with a simple and final diagnosis of bad bruising. It felt good to wake up the next morning to a somewhat normal routine. I walked downstairs to let the dogs out, and for the first time I noticed Tiffani's doll lying in the dirt where Tiffani had fallen. I picked it up and went inside. Later that afternoon while I was talking to Tiffani about the accident, I asked her how she had fallen. She told me that she had made her baby doll fly like Chauncey and Tetet, and that the doll had fallen over the balcony. I looked at her seriously and, for the first time, tried to explain to her that Chauncey and Tetet were not real but rather were imaginary friends.

Tiffani was emphatic. She said, "No, Mommy, they are real and they play with me every day. They are my friends." I asked her what they looked like, and she replied, "They look like me but Chauncey has pink hair and Tetet has white hair and they have no feet, they just fly."

At this point, I was quite intrigued with what she was telling me. When I asked her why or how she had fallen off the balcony, she said that she was trying to get her baby doll. I asked her if she was scared while she was falling, and she said, "No, Mommy, Chauncey and Tetet helped to catch me after I fell off so I wouldn't get hurt."

A few days later, my mother had a similar discussion with Tiffani, and she repeated exactly the same account she had told me about her friends helping her. A few days later, Tiffani told me that Tetet had gone back to the mountains, but Chauncey stayed around for a couple more weeks and then returned to the mountains.

Tiffani is now five and very rarely talks about the incident. Chauncey and Tetet haven't been around for a long time, but I now believe they were with us for a time for a specific purpose. Tiffani came through the accident with one bruise the size of a dime on her left leg and a bad stomachache. I'm quite sure that if it hadn't been for her two loving guardian angels, her injuries would have been much more serious, and perhaps she wouldn't be with us today.

I hope the day will come when I can thank Chauncey and Tetet face-to-face for preserving the life of my precious daughter, and for giving me the privilege of being her mother a while longer.

— TERI JOHNSTON
Salt Lake City, Utah

Picnic Day

I T WAS A Kodak moment—a beautiful sunny California day, green lawns covered with picnic blankets and lawn chairs, the air filled with the happy laughter of children. Parents stood by, watching their offspring with pride. It hardly seemed to matter that the lush green lawn lay in the shade of an enormous hospital. Sutter Memorial Hospital is known throughout Northern California as the premier neonatal center, where dangerously premature babies from all over the state are sent to be cared for by the top specialists in the field. So many of these tiny babies pull through the dramatic circumstances of their births that the hospital has long had a traditional reunion for the babies—their "Sutter Sweethearts." My daughter, Paige, was a Sutter Sweetheart, and that was why she and I attended the picnic that day.

The annual reunion always received good coverage from

the local media. Happy, healthy survivors—and especially young ones—always make for a good story, I guess, and this year was no exception. Not long after we arrived I felt a tap on my shoulder. It was a reporter from a local radio station. She explained that one of the nurses had pointed me out and said that I had a particularly good story to tell. Could she interview me about the circumstances of Paige's birth? So I stood there on the lawn and recounted what had happened to me in the hospital some five years earlier.

After I spent six weeks of bed rest in the hospital, Paige was born three months early, weighing in at only one pound twelve ounces. The doctors soon told us that she had suffered a severe intercranial bleed, causing both a stroke and hydrocephalus (water on the brain), as well as cerebral palsy. She might never walk or talk. How could my husband, Monte, and I care for a baby with such severe medical problems? Did we have the strength and courage her life would require of us?

As I told my story to the reporter, I relived some of the bittersweet emotions of those first few days with Paige—fear, despair, hope, and overwhelming love for this tiny new baby. "We did have the strength and courage," I told the reporter. Not only did we have the courage, but we also had a beautiful daughter who was a joy in our lives. I reached down and rested my hand on Paige's small shoulder. "Not a day goes by that I don't rejoice in her presence."

All the while I was talking with the reporter I had been aware of a young couple standing nearby. They seemed to lean forward and strain to hear every word of my story, and they studied Paige closely as she stood by my side throughout the interview. When the reporter turned off her tape recorder and began to pack up her equipment, they approached.

A young couple in their early twenties, they had faces etched with fear and exhaustion, in sharp contrast to the happy faces of the other people at the party. "We've been listening to what you said to that woman," they said. They pointed up to a second-floor window in the hospital. "Our new son, Joe Jr., is up in the neonatal unit right now. He was born prematurely a week ago." His condition, they explained, was exactly the same as Paige's had been—even the bleed in his brain was the same grade of severity. "The doctors suspect that hydrocephalus is developing, and cerebral palsy might be evident, too." I patted the woman's arm, trying to comfort her. I knew exactly what she was going through.

A year passed, and I often wondered about that young couple and their little baby. Had he lived? As the Sutter Sweetheart reunion drew near again I looked forward to attending and hoped that I would see them there.

I looked everywhere that afternoon, with no luck. Oblivious to the brightly colored balloons and crepe paper decorations, I focused on my search, describing the couple and their baby to every nurse there, but no one could help me, as I didn't know their name. Finally the afternoon drew to a close, and Paige and I packed up our things and walked back to our car.

As we piled our picnic basket and lawn chairs into the back of the trunk, a van pulled into the parking space next to us. A baby peered out the window from his car seat. I glanced up over my shoulder at the driver and recognized him right away. It was the young couple I'd met the year before!

The baby's mother jumped down from her seat in the van and rushed toward me with her arms outstretched. She embraced me warmly—"I'm so glad I found you! I'm so glad I found you!" Her husband unbuckled the boy from his car seat and carried him over to where we all stood.

"This is my son, Joe Jr. Last year, the day we met you, we were in a state of shock. We had just been advised by the doctors that there was little hope for Joe Jr.'s survival, and that we should give them permission, as an act of love and compassion, to disconnect his life support. We were tormented by the decision before us. But then we met you and saw Paige, and we knew what we should do. We told the doctors no. And here he is today, alive and active. We still have many challenges ahead of us, but your courageous example saved our baby's life, and for that we will be eternally grateful.

"We'll never regret the decision that resulted from meeting you that spring day—a meeting we know, that was much more than a mere coincidence."

—SUSAN WHITEFIELD
Granite Bay, California

A Touch of Gold

I saw it as a sign, a heavenly gift—perhaps a symbol of the gold, frankincense, and myrrh that were the original gifts of Christmas. Others saw it merely as a happy accident, but I knew in my heart it was a message of hope for my little family.

It was early December and I had just returned home after another exhausting day at work as a waitress in our small town's café. As a recently divorced mother of two, I was working six days a week to make ends meet, but even with tips, I was barely able to keep up with the bills. My daughters, Cristen, age ten, and Jamie, age seven, were getting older and needing more and more. Pneumonia had rocked our family budget the year before, and I worried that the girls wouldn't be able to have the things other kids had. Cristen played in the school band, and clarinets weren't cheap. And now the Christmas season was upon us, the shopping frenzy was already in overdrive, and I had been thinking a lot about how I would manage to put anything under the tree for them. No parent in the world wants their kids to lose the magic anticipation of Christmas.

We live in a small community of five hundred people—an old mining town as rich in history as it once was in gold. There are wonderful old artifacts all around the area that my family loves to collect—driftwood, old shovels, pans used to sift for gold, pinecones, unique little jars, rocks, dried flowers. I have a collection of pretty rocks, some of which belonged to my great-grandmother. So in that same family tradition, my two daughters are always bringing interesting little things home to add to our collection. And like most parents, I always save them.

On that particular night, I had just cooked dinner and the girls were finishing their homework. From across the room Cristen casually said, "Hey, Mom, see this rock I found today?" I told her it looked interesting and asked her to bring it over to me. When I looked at it up close I was dumbfounded. I'd worked in mines when I was young—I used to help my grandfather set the dynamite—and I knew you didn't just find these things lying around. It was about one and a half inches long, and its shape reminded me of a little giraffe. I thought I was seeing things and asked Cristen where she found it. She told me she found it when she was playing in a pile of dirt outside her school.

I immediately ran down the street to my mother's house, threw open the door, and said, "Tell me this is what I know it is!" The rock was a one-ounce gold nugget, probably worth somewhere between $300 and $400. A jeweler or rock hound might pay twice that. Idaho City's mines had once produced more gold than all of Alaska. Its gold had financed the Union Army during the Civil War. But the odds of finding a nugget this large on a school playground were unheard of.

When our little miracle finally hit the news, Jack Lyman, Idaho Mining Association director, said, "I've been here nine years and have never heard of anything like it happening anywhere."

I was able to buy some toys for the girls that Christmas and some new clothes they needed badly. But the incident brought more than gifts under the tree. It reminded us that there was someone watching over us, someone we can put our trust in, and someone whose love can turn even the most cynical hearts heavenward.

Our miracle did another wonderful thing shortly after Christmas. My mother has suffered from a degenerative disk disease for many years. She has had five surgeries and has gone back and forth to a hospital in Boise many times. Now a doctor in Texas wanted to do a new form of laser treatment that he felt would finally relieve her painful condition. With the money left over from the sale of our gold nugget, I was able to buy my mother the plane ticket to Texas.

We will not forget our miracle or the happiness it brought two little girls on Christmas Day and the opportunity to give their grandmother the gift she sorely needed. But most of all, our little gold nugget gave us a glimmer of hope in a weary world and a reason to keep believing.

— GWEN ELLIS
Idaho City, Idaho

Expect a Miracle, Mama

HEN I MOVED from a big city to a small town in Texas, I felt a little out of place. The residents of Pampa were down-home, simple country folk, and the one thing they were all proud of was the beautiful gardens in each of their backyards. In an attempt to join with my new community, I decided it was time to plant a garden of my own. This was a new endeavor for me, so when one of my neighbors recommended using compost, which I could get free from the city landfill, I decided to give it a try.

I loaded up our new van with my four children, a shovel, three buckets, and a plastic bag, and headed over to the landfill. As soon as I pulled up and opened my door, I was hit by a gust of wind, and one of my contact lenses flew out of my eye. I could think of only two things at that moment: one, that finding a contact in a compost pile had to be at least as difficult as finding a needle in a haystack, and two, that finding the three hundred dollars for a new set of contacts and an eye exam might even be harder than that! Still determined to get the compost, however, I loaded it up, keeping my one eye closed so I could focus.

The events of the next hour made me wonder if I would ever measure up to my "green-thumbed" neighbors. I dragged the plastic bag full of compost into our yard, not knowing there was a hole in the bottom, and left a dirty trail from inside our new van all the way to the backyard. Eager to get the compost on my garden, I started putting it around every plant by hand. Naturally, one of the times I reached into the bucket, I picked up a big, squishy cow patty. Then as I stepped across one of the wooden planks outlining my beds, it skidded across the mud like a surfboard, and I fell flat into the garden doing the splits! As I sat in the mud, my frustration turned to hysteria and I began laughing uncontrollably. My children looked at me as though I had lost my mind, and I believe we were all feeling that it was time to head back to the big city.

Trying to divert all of our attention to something more constructive, I asked the children to help me search the van to see if the wind had blown my contact lens inside it somewhere. We searched the floorboards, the seats, the ashtray, every nook and cranny. We couldn't find it anywhere. I finally resigned myself to the fact that it was gone for good. Sensing my discouragement, each of my kids told me they were sorry we had had such a bad day. It certainly was one of the worst since our move. Maybe I was just struggling too hard to fit into a town in which I really didn't belong. I was lonely—I missed my family and friends. Why had we moved here, anyway? Privately, I questioned God, asking what He was trying to tell me. I begged Him to make it known to me.

The night was over and I was tired. I went to each of my children to say good night. When I got to my nine-year-old son, Trey, he looked up at me and said, "Mama, do you believe in miracles?" Not wanting to crush the faith of a child, I responded, "I sure do!" And he said, "Well, why haven't we had any miracles in our life?"

I suddenly realized what a disservice I was doing to my children by sulking over something as trivial as a contact lens. So I proceeded to tell him some of the wonderful miracles and blessings we had received in our life. Like the time he was a nine-month-old baby in Texas Children's Hospital with a 106-degree temperature, and the doctors didn't know what was wrong. After a week of tests and observation they determined that Trey probably had a birth defect that would require surgery. Before going in for a final test, I said a quick prayer, and off we went to the X-ray room. I held my little baby down during the X-rays, with tears streaming down my face. We went back into the room to wait for the results. The doctor came in smiling and said, "You got your miracle. No surgery will be necessary. Everything is working as it should. You can go home now." I explained to Trey that this was indeed a wonderful miracle, but that he was just too young to remember it.

Then he said, "Mama, maybe if we pray to God, you'll get a miracle and find your contact lens." Of course. Such a simple solution to a child. Why did faith always seem so much more complicated to adults? Needing his strength, I said, "Will you pray with me?" So we did. Trey led us in a wonderful prayer straight from a child's innocent heart. Right afterward he turned to me and said, "Mama, did you check your purse?"

All of a sudden, I remembered that my purse had been sitting open by the driver's seat when I got out of the van at the compost pile. I ran to my bedroom to get my purse. Trey and I plopped down on the living room floor. We spread out a sheet to catch all of the articles as I dumped it out. My husband was lying on the couch after a hard day of work and looked over at us. Puzzled, he said, "What on earth are you doing?" I smiled at Trey and said, "We're finding my contact lens. We have reason to believe it's in here." I searched meticulously through the pile on the floor, but once again, I found no lens.

In a last-ditch effort, I picked up the empty purse and peeked inside. To my amazement, there it was on the bottom, safe and sound. Trey and I rejoiced at our miracle, and I immediately put it safely away in its case.

I was deeply touched by this very simple event that proved to me the power of a child's faith. So often, children are God's answer to our depression, discouragement, and loneliness. But more than that, while we are busy teaching them how to be adults, they are teaching us how to be children. And the longer I live, the more I realize the strength of that quality—"to become as a little child."

Because of the example of a small child, my faith continues to grow and flourish. And incidentally, so does my garden.

—TINA COLIGAN-HOLT
Pampa, Texas

Do you have a miracle you would like to share? We are putting together more books about miracles. We would love to hear about the miracle in your life. Please send your story to:

JENNIFER BASYE SANDER

BIG CITY BOOKS

"MIRACLES"

P.O. BOX 2463

GRANITE BAY, CA

95746-2463

Please include your address and phone number so we can contact you.

Acknowledgments

As always, our warmest thanks and deepest gratitude to the talented people at William Morrow, especially our dedicated editor, Toni Sciarra, and associate editor, Katharine Cluverius. We are also thankful to our agent, Sheree Bykofsky, for making this book a reality.

No book is complete without the contributions of others. We sincerely thank the following for their time, effort, and support:

Xan Albright, Vivian Antrim, Lindsay Artsten, Kerstin Backman, Anne Basye, the Basye family, Linda Blackhurst, Daryl Bohnstedt, Linda Wenker Boutin, Bill Burch, Patricia Cameransi, Liane Carter, Diane Cawthon, Jane Stratford Clayson, Tina Coligan-Holt, Donna Conkling, Nettie Conlon, Cynthia Stewart Cooper, Sherry Crum, Sarah Rizzolo Curci, Cookie Curci-Wright, Mary Jeane Davis, Ginni Lopez De Holien, Melinda Ehlers, Gwen Ellis, *The Ensign* magazine,

ACKNOWLEDGMENTS

Surie Fettman, Rocco Francisco, Hope Gardner, the Glassover family, Diane Goldberg, Nancy Hafers, Raelene Hill, Hilary Hinckley, Azriela Jaffe, Teri Johnston, Maureen Keeney, Jo Kopfer, August Kund, Marianna Laney, Linda Lee, the Lewis family, Kristin Peterson Linton, Chris Lloyd, Cathy Lonsdale, Maria Guadalupe Lopez, Angie Mangino, Diane S. Matthews, Roberta Messner, the Miller family, Amy Nihan, Chuck Patton, Ellen Patton, Julie Price, Jill E. Reed, Amber M. Reilly, Debbie Rhodes, Rosemarie Riley, Sheila Shatzer, Marion Roach Smith, Rich Strasser, the Sander family, Joni Taylor, Susie Wagner, Marian Jeppson Walker, Laurette Walton, Donna Weber, Susan Whitefield, Sarah Hanks Wilcox, Kris Wilkes, Amy Wolford, Dr. Joan LeSueur Woods, and Lynne Zielinski.